Praise for *How Do Catholics Read the Bible?*

"Dan Harrington has the uncanny ability to make the complex, understandable and the profound, accessible to ordinary readers. In this volume, he brings together wise reflections on methods of interpreting Scripture today with examples from his own experience of interpreting Scripture for parish communities. *How do Catholics Read the Bible?* is a reliable guide for every Catholic who has waited for a straightforward and clearly written introduction to reading the Bible in the Church today."

—**Barbara E. Bowe**, R.S.C.J.,
Professor of Biblical Studies, Catholic Theological Union,

"A splendid companion to the Bible. A sure guide through issues that need to be understood if the reader is to appreciate how the Bible is 'the Word of God in human language.'"

—**Emil A. Wcela**, Auxiliary Bishop, Diocese of Rockville Centre and past President, Catholic Biblical Association

"Harrington's book is a wonderfully clear, balanced, and accessible presentation of how the Catholic Church at its best understands and uses the Bible. Always user-friendly, this book should prove helpful for a wide audience of Catholics and others who are interested in understanding the Bible in its historical contexts and, even more importantly, in their daily lives and in the life of the Church today. The book obviously reflects Harrington's thirty years of teaching, preaching, and praying over the biblical text."

—**Thomas H. Tobin, S.J.**,
Professor of Theology, Loyola University Chicago

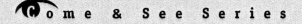
Come & See Series

The **Come & See Series** from Sheed & Ward is modeled on Jesus' compassionate question: "What do you seek?" and his profound invitation to "Come and see" the world through the eyes of faith (John 1:38–39). The series offers spiritual seekers lively, thought-provoking, and accessible books that explore topics of faith and the Catholic Christian tradition. Each book in the series is written by trustworthy guides who are the very best teachers, theologians, and scholars.

Series Editors: James Martin, S.J., and Jeremy Langford

People of the Covenant: An Invitation to the Old Testament
By Dianne Bergant

Who is Jesus? Why is He Important?: An Invitation to the New Testament
By Daniel J. Harrington, S.J.

Living Justice: Catholic Social Teaching in Action
By Thomas Massaro, S.J.

Professions of Faith: Living and Working as a Catholic
Edited by James Martin, S.J., and Jeremy Langford

A Faith You Can Live With: Understanding the Basics
By John O'Donnell, S.J.

Bread of Life, Cup of Salvation: Understanding the Mass
By John Baldovin, S.J.

How Do Catholics Read the Bible?
By Daniel J. Harrington, S.J.

HOW DO CATHOLICS
READ THE BIBLE?

Daniel J. Harrington, S.J.

A Sheed & Ward Book

ROWMAN & LITTLEFIELD PUBLISHERS, INC.

Lanham • Boulder • New York • Toronto • Oxford

A SHEED & WARD BOOK

ROWMAN & LITTLEFIELD PUBLISHERS, INC.

Published in the United States of America
by Rowman & Littlefield Publishers, Inc.
A wholly owned subsidary of The Rowman & Littlefield Publishing Group, Inc.
4501 Forbes Boulevard, Suite 200, Lanham, Maryland 20706
www.rowmanlittlefield.com

PO Box 317
Oxford
OX2 9RU, UK

British Library Cataloguing in Publication Information Available

Library of Congress Cataloging-in-Publication Data

Harrington, Daniel J.
    How do Catholics read the Bible? / Daniel J. Harrington.
        p. cm. — (Come & see series)
    "A Sheed & Ward book."
    Includes bibliographical references and index.
    ISBN 0-7425-4870-8 (cloth : alk. paper) — ISBN 0-7425-4871-6 (pbk.
: alk. paper)
    1. Bible—Reading. 2. Bible—Hermeneutics. 3. Bible—Study and teach-
ing—Catholic Church. 4. Catholic Church—Doctrines. I. Title. II. Series:
Come & see.

    BS617.H36 2005
    220'.088'282—dc22   2004030452

Printed in the United States of America

♾ᵀᴹ The paper used in this publication meets the minimum requirements of
American National Standard for Information Sciences—Permanence of Paper
for Printed Library Materials, ANSI/NISO Z39.48-1992.

In Memory of

Rev. Frederick L. Moriarty, S.J. (1913–2004)

Mentor and Friend

Contents

Introduction

Around 1950, when I was ten years old, two well-dressed gentlemen came to our house. They rang the doorbell, and my mother answered. I was nearby and overheard the conversation. They introduced themselves as "ministers of Christ" and asked if they might come in and discuss the Bible with us. My mother gave them the response that most good Catholics of that time would have given: "We're Catholics. We don't read the Bible." The conversation was over.

In fact Catholics then did read the Bible. Only most of them probably did not realize it. Whenever they attended Mass, the Scriptures were read. But the texts were in Latin, and most people could understand them only if they had an English translation known as a "missal." It is safe to say, however, that not many Catholics around 1950 (apart from some priests and monks) spent a lot of time reading the Bible.

That incident intrigued me. I wanted to know why Catholics did not read the Bible. Around the same time I read in a newspaper that according to the book of Exodus Moses stuttered. I did, too, and so I was eager to find out if what was in the newspaper article was true. And so I got hold of a Bible (the Douay version, which was the approved Catholic version of the time, of course) and found in Exodus 4:10 that Moses resisted God's call to lead his people and to plead with Pharaoh for their liberation from slavery in Egypt on the grounds that "I am slow of speech and slow of tongue."

This verse is part of the narrative in Exodus 3–4 about Moses' experience of God on Mount Horeb and his call to lead God's people. It is one of the greatest texts in the Bible. The passage as a whole contains all the dynamics of religious experience: the numinous burning bush, Moses' curiosity and fear, the concept of holy ground, the call from God, the self-revelation of God, the commission to go to the land promised to Abraham and his descendants, God's promise to bring about these things, displays of miraculous power on Moses' part, his continued resistance to accepting the call, and his final acceptance of it.

Moses' speech problem (whatever it was) is put into perspective when God says to him: "Who gives speech to mortals? . . . Is it not I, the Lord?" (Exod 4:11). This biblical passage remains the most important biblical text in my life not so much for what it says about Moses' speech problem, but rather for what it says about my experience of God and my lifelong efforts to live in relationship with God.

I entered the Society of Jesus (Jesuits) in 1958. A few years later, I received from my dean of studies the best advice anyone ever gave me. He said: "You should go into biblical studies. It's the coming field." In the early 1960s biblical studies was indeed the coming field in Roman Catholic circles, due in large part to Pope Pius XII's encyclical on promoting biblical studies (*Divino afflante Spiritu*). Although that document was promulgated in 1943, it only began to make much of an impact in the 1950s, after World War II had ended. I began to read some of the new books and articles, especially from France, where many well-trained theologians had seen the need to get back to the ancient sources of Christian faith such as the Bible and the Church Fathers. And so I was sold on biblical studies.

To go on in biblical studies I had to learn many ancient and modern languages, which I did with enthusiasm and pleasure. To be able to read the Greek New Testament and the Hebrew Bible I found to be a privilege and a thrill. In my basic studies at Weston Jesuit School of Theology and in my doctoral program at Harvard University (1965–69) as well as in periods of study at the Hebrew University in Jerusalem and at the Ecole Biblique de Jérusalem, I had the very best biblical professors—Catholic, Protestant, and Jewish—of their generation. From them I learned to read the Bible both critically and reverently.

Since my ordination to the Catholic priesthood in 1971, I have taught biblical studies at Weston Jesuit School of Theology in Cambridge and occasionally at other institutions. I love to teach about the Bible. I am not sure that I would do well or be happy in teaching history or mathematics or English. It is not so much the teaching that delights me as it is what I teach: biblical languages, individual books of the Bible, introductions to the New Testament, seminars in biblical theology, postexilic Jewish history, the Dead Sea Scrolls, and so forth.

Through the years I have written more than thirty books and hundreds of articles and book reviews pertaining to the Bible. Some are for general audiences like this book, while others are very technical studies of ancient texts (Pseudo-Philo's *Biblical Antiquities*, Qumran wisdom texts, and so on). I have been associated with *New Testament Abstracts* for over forty years and have served as general editor for over thirty years. Each year this journal provides objective summaries of more than two thousand articles and eight hundred books in many languages. I get to see practically everything published in my field. I have also edited and contributed to the Sacra Pagina series of New Testament commentaries (Liturgical Press), the first full-scale Catholic commentary in English. With my mentor and friend John Strugnell, I worked on the edition of a very large Hebrew wisdom text (known as 4Q Instruction) found among the Dead Sea Scrolls for the official Discoveries in the Judaean Desert series. And I have preached every Sunday on the Scriptures at local parishes since 1971. The Bible has been my life.

Early in my research for this book I came across a quotation from St. Jerome in Pope Pius XII's 1943 encyclical *Divino afflante Spiritu* that impressed me greatly: "To live amidst these things [biblical studies], to meditate on these things, to know nothing else, to seek nothing else, does it not seem to you already here below a foretaste of the heavenly kingdom?" (*Letters* 53 [to Paulinus] 10). This statement expresses perfectly what has been the story of my life with the Bible.

In this volume I want to explain to nonspecialist readers what I regard as the basic dimensions of a Catholic approach to reading and interpreting the Bible. Without overloading the text with quotations and references, I will try to give a positive and constructive presentation very much in the spirit of Vatican II's *Dei verbum* (1965) and the Pontifical Biblical Commission's 1993 instruction on "The Interpretation of the Bible in the Church."

Each of the eight chapters will begin with a short quotation from *Dei verbum*, discuss the main topic in three sections (see the table of contents), and conclude with three questions for reflection and discussion. A short annotated bibliography on modern Catholic biblical scholarship and a glossary are also included. My hope is that readers of this book may come to know and love the Scriptures as I do and find in them (as Jerome did) "a foretaste of the heavenly kingdom."

What Do Catholics Believe about the Bible?

"For the words of God, expressed in human language, have become like unto human speech, just as the Word of the eternal Father, when he took on himself the flesh of human weakness, became like unto human beings." (Dei verbum 13)

Christianity is sometimes described alongside Judaism and Islam as a "religion of the book." However, that description is not entirely accurate, since Christianity is really the religion of a person, Jesus Christ, the Word of God, to whom the words in the church's book (the Bible) bear witness. Or better still, Christianity is the religion of God understood and experienced as Father, Son, and Holy Spirit. The Bible, or

Holy Scripture, the book that both created the church and was created by the church, is a privileged witness to the triune God's dealings with the people of God in both Old and New Testaments.

From the very beginning, the Bible and the church have existed in a circular or even symbiotic relationship. After sketching the early history of that relationship, I will describe where one can best find what Catholics today believe about the Bible in some recent official Catholic Church documents. Then I will focus on the expression "the word of God in human language" as especially expressive of the Catholic approach to the Bible and its interpretation.

The Bible and the Church

The term *symbiosis* refers to two entities (groups, persons, organisms, etc.) living together and cooperating in a mutually beneficial relationship. Throughout history, the Bible and the church have had a symbiotic relationship. The Holy Scriptures read by Jesus and the earliest Christians were what Christians today call the Old Testament. Jesus formulated his wise teachings and talked about himself and God's kingdom largely in the language and conceptuality of the Jewish Scriptures. After Jesus' death and resurrection, the early Christians interpreted what happened to Jesus in light of those Scriptures and found him to be the key that opened up their "true" or "full" meaning in relation to the life, death, and resurrection of Jesus. The Holy Scriptures of Israel constituted the Bible of the earliest church. To a large extent the Old Testament provided that church with the vocabulary and concepts for early Christian efforts at theology.

While the Bible played an important role in creating the church, the church played a vital role in creating its own

Bible consisting of both Old and New Testaments. The process of canonization of Christian books seems to have started when Paul's letters were copied and read in churches other than those that they originally addressed, and began to be collected together in some kind of packets and sent around from church to church. The four Gospels (attributed to Matthew, Mark, Luke, and John) with their distinctive portraits of Jesus soon also came to enjoy a privileged status among early Christians, along with the Acts of the Apostles (by Luke) and the other writings eventually classed among the New Testament epistles. These books too were put into final form in and for specific communities, often addressing the pastoral needs of those communities. They too were copied and circulated around to other Christian communities in Italy, Greece, Asia Minor (present-day Turkey), Syria, and Palestine. All of these New Testament books emerged out of church life in the first Christian century. All of them responded to crises or needs that early Christians were experiencing. But they soon came to transcend the immediate circumstances of their composition and to be read and appreciated in new situations. They were eventually recognized for their great wisdom and spiritual value among Christians as having been written under the guidance and inspiration of the Holy Spirit.

Between the second and fourth Christian centuries there was widespread acceptance of the four Gospels and Paul's letters as somehow authoritative in the sense of providing a *canon* (the term means "measuring stick") for Christian faith and practice. While there were disputes about some other books (in both the Old and New Testaments), by the late fourth century most early Christians recognized as authoritative the books in the wider collection of the Greek translation of the Old Testament books (called the "Septuagint") made by Jews in Alexandria of Egypt from the third century B.C. onward and widely used by Jews and early Christians outside the land of Israel, and the books in the now traditional New Testament corpus. These books in turn were viewed as providing the "measuring stick" or norm by which the church could and did judge its theology and practice.

So from the very beginning the Bible and the church have been in a symbiotic relationship. The Bible that we know as the Old Testament was a major factor in shaping the vocabulary and thought of Jesus and the early Christians. The early Christians began to produce their own writings that eventually came to be accepted as part of their own Holy Scriptures as "the New Testament." The church under the guidance of the Holy Spirit recognized and decided what books belonged in its canon of Christian Scripture. And that canon in turn has served as the rule or norm of faith and practice for the church.

Modern Catholic Documentation

The Roman Catholic Church has official documents about practically everything. But the nature of the Bible and how to interpret it have been topics of special importance and concern for over a hundred years. These matters have been treated in the form of a dogmatic constitution from the Second Vatican Council (1965), two long papal encyclicals (1893, 1943), two major documents issued by the Pontifical Biblical Commission (1964, 1993), and other official pronouncements. All these documents have been collected, translated, and edited by Dean Béchard, S.J., in *The Scripture Documents: An Anthology of Official Catholic Teachings*.[1]

Here I will focus on the five documents mentioned above and treat them in the chronological order of their publication. The effect of these documents is cumulative, in the sense that one builds upon another. The later documents take over the main points from the earlier ones and even cite them as authoritative sources. At the same time each new document reflects its own historical setting and makes new points that have become part of the Catholic Church's authoritative teachings on the Bible and how to interpret it.

An encyclical is a letter from the bishop of Rome (the pope) to the whole Catholic Church or even to the whole world. An encyclical usually treats doctrinal, moral, or social issues that the pope feels are in urgent need of clarification. The term *encyclical* reflects the ancient practice of letters being sent around to a "circle" (*kyklos* in Greek) of communities. The New Testament books known as Ephesians, 1 Peter, and Revelation were likely addressed and sent to such a circle of churches. The practice of the bishop of Rome writing encyclicals has become especially prominent in the past 125 years. The modern papal encyclicals and most other Roman church documents are generally known by their first few Latin words.

Pope Leo XIII's 1893 encyclical letter on the study of Scripture is known as *Providentissimus Deus* ("The God of all Providence"). It was intended chiefly to respond to European rationalists who were using "critical" (in the negative sense) methods of reading Scripture and the findings of "natural science" to deny the possibility of divine revelation and to dismiss the truth of the Bible. By all admissions (even Pope John Paul II) the tone of this encyclical is defensive and apologetic (that is, meant to defend or prove the truth of Christian doctrine). Nevertheless, *Providentissimus Deus* made many positive points that have become part of later official Catholic teachings about the Bible and its interpretation: the divine origin of the Scriptures, the positive value of the history of biblical interpretation, the inerrancy of Scripture, the primacy of the literal sense and the legitimacy of the spiritual sense, the contributions made by studying biblical and ancient Near Eastern languages and cultures, the need for well-trained biblical scholars, and the importance of the Bible in every phase of church life.

Pope Pius XII's 1943 encyclical letter promoting biblical studies is referred to as *Divino afflante Spiritu* ("Inspired by the Divine Spirit"). Though intended to commemorate the fiftieth anniversary of Pope Leo XIII's *Providentissimus Deus,* its circumstances and tone were quite different. It was written from Rome in the middle of World War II and mentions how "a cruel war heaps ruins upon ruins and slaughter upon slaughter" (28). The more immediate occasion, however, was a pamphlet circulating in the Italian churches that attacked the scientific study of the Bible as a danger to the faith of Catholics.

The encyclical from Pius XII is positive in content and even optimistic in tone. While it repeats many points from *Providentissimus Deus,* the encyclical known as *Divino afflante Spiritu* moved Catholic biblical scholarship forward by embracing the scientific methods being used by Catholics and other biblical scholars. It praises the achievements of archaeologists in illumining the world of the Bible. It points to progress in the study of ancient languages, textual criticism, and philology. It emphasizes the importance of establishing the literal sense of biblical texts as the foundation for drawing out their spiritual sense(s). It insists on the need to determine "the peculiar character and circumstances of the sacred writer, the age in which he lived, the sources written and oral to which he had recourse, and the forms of expression he employed" (19). It stresses the value of entering into "the mentality of ancient writers, as well as their manner and art of reasoning, narrating, and writing" (22). In particular, it recommends that special attention be given to the study of the literary forms or "the modes of speaking and writing in use among the ancients" (21) as a way of understanding better the truth of the Bible. This encyclical from Pope Pius XII set in motion full Catholic participation in modern biblical scholarship, while insisting on the Bible as the word of God and on biblical study as a theological discipline.

The Pontifical Biblical Commission is an international group of Catholic biblical scholars chosen by the Vatican to offer their learning and advice on matters pertaining to the Bible and its interpretation. In 1964 the Commission issued its "Instruction on the Historical Truth of the Gospels" known as *Sancta Mater Ecclesia* ("Holy Mother the Church"). The occasion was the confusion being caused by interpretations of the Gospels emanating from several different sources: rationalists who dismissed the possibility of divine revelation and the supernatural realm, liberal Protestant theologians who claimed that faith has no connection to historical truth, others who denied the historical character and value of the biblical writings, and still others who suggested that the church made up most of what appears in the Gospels.

In response to these many aberrations, the Commission insisted on the positive value of the scientific methods outlined in Pope Pius XII's encyclical. It also contended that to be understood properly the Gospels must be read and interpreted at three levels or stages in the process of their transmission and composition: Jesus (A.D. 30), the earliest churches

(30–70), and the Evangelists who put the Gospels into their final forms (70–100). While assuming a basic continuity throughout the three stages, the document also indicates the distinctive contributions that were made at each level. It notes especially the many literary forms (catechesis, narratives, testimonies, hymns, doxologies, prayers, and so on) that the tradition about Jesus took in the early church and the constructive role played by the Gospel writers in integrating these traditions into their narratives and in responding to the pastoral needs of Christians in their own times.

The most synthetic and authoritative Catholic statement on the Bible and its interpretation comes from the Second Vatican Council held in Rome from 1962 to 1965. This was an ecumenical council made up of Catholic bishops and their theological advisers from all over the world (which is the root meaning of *ecumenical*). The first such council since the end of Vatican I in 1870, Vatican II was unprecedented in its invitation to non-Catholic "observers" and in the interest that it created in the popular media. It was convoked by Pope John XXIII to be a pastoral council, with a special concern for bringing the Catholic Church "up to date" (*aggiornamento* in Italian).

Among the many documents produced at Vatican II, one of the most important is the Dogmatic Constitution on Divine Revelation known as *Dei verbum* ("the Word of God"). Any dogmatic constitution emanating from an ecumenical council is an official document enjoying the highest authority. This document went through several drafts. Indeed, the rejection of its first draft marked a decisive moment in the history of Vatican II. That first draft was a rather traditional and defensive restatement of scholastic theology on divine revelation, more in tune with *Providentissimus Deus* (1893) than with *Divino afflante Spiritu* (1943), as we've discussed above. Many of the council participants wished to move forward on the topic and to respond better to the needs of their time.

The version of *Dei verbum* that emerged from what was a long and often difficult editorial process remains the most authoritative source for learning what Catholics believe about the Bible. Like all the council's documents, *Dei verbum* is a balanced and carefully nuanced composition. It deliberately stands in the tradition of the papal encyclicals and the instruction on the historical truth of the Gospels. It frequently adopts their wording and makes many references to them in its footnotes. It is expressed in such a way that it won near universal approval from the bishops participating in the council. It is a consensus document, not representing any one school of Catholic theology or resolving matters of serious theological dispute.

Dei verbum consists of six chapters. They treat revelation itself, the transmission of divine revelation, the divine inspiration of Scripture and its interpretation, the Old Testament, the New Testament, and Sacred Scripture in the life of the church. Since this book deals with all these topics and makes frequent references to *Dei verbum,* here I will mention only a few "highlights" in the document. What follows are some ways in which *Dei verbum* integrates the key insights of the earlier documents and offers new perspectives about the Bible and its interpretation today.

Dei verbum is important first of all for its insistence on the primacy of God's personal self-revelation: "It has pleased God in his goodness and wisdom to reveal himself and to make known the mystery of his will" (2). Another significant development appears in the treatment of the relationship between Scripture and tradition, which has long been a topic of theological controversy between Catholics and Protestants. While holding firm in its defense of tradition as a source of divine revelation, the document emphasizes the close relationship between Scripture and tradition, and describes them as "flowing from the same divine wellspring" (9).

This conciliar document also balances the need to investigate the historical context and literary form of biblical texts (historical criticism) with a strong statement on the need to read and interpret Scripture "in the light of the same Spirit by whom it was written" (12). It also emphasizes the lasting value of the Old Testament books. While admitting that in some respects these books contain "what is only incomplete and provisional, nevertheless [they] demonstrate God's true way of instructing" (15). In treating the Gospels, *Dei verbum* makes its own the idea of three stages in the development of the Gospels—Jesus, the early church, and the Evangelists—described in *Sancta Mater Ecclesia* (1964). In dealing with the place of the Bible in church life, *Dei verbum* as part of a "pastoral" council is even more vigorous than the earlier documents in its insistence that all the faithful must have easy access to the Scriptures and that the Bible must play a central role in all areas of theology ("the soul of theology") and church practice (catechesis, liturgy, etc.).

Providentissimus Deus appeared in 1893, and *Divino afflante Spiritu* was published in 1943. It was anticipated that another papal encyclical on the Bible would be forthcoming in 1993. But rather than continuing the encyclical tradition, Pope John Paul II charged the Pontifical Biblical Commission with writing a document on "The Interpretation of the Bible in the Church."[2] Whereas the earlier documents were mainly concerned with explaining what the Bible is, this statement issued in 1993 focuses almost entirely on how to interpret the Bible. It aims "to attend to the criticisms and the complaints, as also to the hopes and aspirations that are being expressed in this matter, to assess the possibilities opened up by the new methods and approaches, and, finally, to try to determine more precisely the direction that best corresponds to the mission of exegesis in the Catholic church" (Introduction B.).

Between Vatican II and the publication of this document, the Pontifical Biblical Commission underwent some changes in its mission and a restructuring. The group that prepared the document consisted of about twenty eminent Catholic biblical exegetes from various parts of the world. The Commission now works on topics of special concern to the pope and to the Congregation for the Doctrine of the Faith. It is an advisory or consultative body, and its documents do not have the official ecclesial authority that council documents and papal encyclicals have. However, this particular document was warmly received by Pope John II in a 1993 address in which he praised its spirit of openness, its balance and moderation, and its contribution to letting the biblical word speak to all humanity.

The Commission's document has four major parts. They deal with methods and approaches for interpretation, hermeneutical questions, characteristics of Catholic interpretation, and interpretation of the Bible in the life of the church. It goes deeply into the process of biblical interpretation and offers balanced judgments on what constitutes biblical exegesis today. It has been positively received not only by Catholics but also by Protestant and Jewish scholars. Along with *Dei verbum,* it provides the most up-to-date and comprehensive source for learning about how Catholics read the Bible today.

The most obvious "highlight" in this document is its extensive descriptions and critical analyses of the methods and approaches currently being used in professional biblical studies. It asserts that the historical-critical method is "the indispensable method for scientific study of the meaning of ancient texts" (I.A), while giving ample scope to the various literary methods employed in studying the texts themselves. It recognizes the positive contributions made by other disciplines such as the social sciences and philosophical hermeneutics, and emphasizes the importance of the interpreter's social setting. It reserves its harshest criticism for fundamentalist interpretation (an excessively literalistic approach to the Bible that pays no attention to its historical circumstances and spiritual or symbolic significance), which it calls "dangerous" on the grounds that it "invites people to a kind of intellectual suicide" because it "injects into life a false certitude" (I.F).

What emerges from our survey of all these official Catholic documents on the Bible and its interpretation is the rich and inclusive nature of the Catholic approach to reading the Bible. The Catholic Church is in fact the most diverse and inclusive institution in the world. True to its name, Catholicism is well represented all over the world, and manages a balance between its elaborate sociological structures and the participation of all kinds of peoples.

At its core Catholicism encourages "both/and" rather than "either/or" thinking. In looking at Scripture the official Catholic documentation insists on both the divine origin of the Bible and the necessary contribution of the human persons who composed the books of the Bible in a certain time and place. It urges interpreters both to respect the spiritual dimensions of the biblical texts and at the same time to use all their human intellectual powers in trying to understand them better. One way to summarize what Catholics believe about the Bible comes in a phrase that runs through several of the official documents. They say that the Bible is "the word of God in human language" (or more literally, "the word of God in the words of men").

The Word of God in Human Language

The quotation from *Dei verbum* 13 printed at the beginning of this chapter uses the analogy of the incarnation of Jesus the Word of God to describe the presence of both divine and human elements in Scripture. Like all analogies, it is not without problems. But it has become a modern (with patristic roots) Catholic way of preserving the traditional understanding of the Bible both as originating with God under the guidance of the Holy Spirit and as put into human language by the biblical writers. Just as Catholics profess Jesus to be fully divine and fully human, so they look upon their Sacred Scriptures as both divine and human.

When biblical texts are read publicly as part of Catholic liturgies, it is customary to introduce each reading by specifying the book from which the passage is taken. The reader says: "A reading from the book of Isaiah," or "A reading from the Holy Gospel according to Matthew." In this way the historical contribution of human beings to "the word of God" is recognized and honored. At the end of each passage, however, the reader adds a tag line and says: "The Gospel of the Lord" for Gospel passages, and "The word of the Lord" for other biblical texts. In this way the divine origin of the biblical text is noted and affirmed. This practice, though hardly even noticed by most Catholics, expresses nicely the Catholic insistence on the Bible as both divine and human.

It is a subtle way of stating that the Bible is the word of God in human language.

The theme of the "word of God" has a rich biblical background. According to Genesis 1, God created the world by his word alone: "And God said. . . ." Likewise by "his word" God sustains and directs everything (Psalm 147:15, 18). Through the prophets God transmits his word to Israel: "Thus says the Lord. . . ." When the Lord touches the mouth of the reluctant prophet Jeremiah, he affirms: "Now I have put my words in your mouth" (1:9). According to Isaiah 55:10–11 the word of God is powerful enough to affect the course of history: "It [my word] shall not return to me empty, but it shall accomplish that which I purpose, and succeed in the things for which I sent it." In the biblical Wisdom Books the connection is made between the word of God and the figure of Wisdom personified. According to Proverbs 8:22–31, Wisdom was present at the creation of the world. According to Sirach 24:3, Wisdom "came forth from the mouth of the Most High." And the book of Wisdom identifies Wisdom as God's "all-powerful word" (18:15).

In these biblical passages the word of God is much more than words written in a book. Rather, the "word of God" describes how God works in the world and in salvation history as the creating, sustaining, directing, and revealing Lord of all. Such texts provide a context for understanding Jesus as the Word of God, and highlight the dynamic and revelatory nature of Scripture as the word of God in human language.

We use words all the time. Indeed the ability to use words is perhaps the most distinctive characteristic of human persons. We speak words; we read words; and we write words. By using words we are able to communicate what we think, and we are able to make others understand what is on our mind, at least most of the time. To call Jesus the Word of God (John 1:1, 14) is to say that he is what God wants to tell us, that Jesus is the revelation of what God wants to say to us and wants us to hear.

Jesus' identity as the Wisdom and Word of God is based on his intimate relationship with his heavenly Father: "No one knows the Son except the Father, and no one knows the Father except the Son and anyone to whom the Son chooses to reveal him" (Matt 11:27). As both the revelation and revealer of God, Jesus is appropriately called the Word of God. In taking on our human nature Jesus became fully human while remaining fully divine: "And the Word was God . . . and the Word became flesh and lived among us" (John 1:1, 14).

The letter to the Hebrews begins by reminding us that while long ago God spoke to our ancestors through the prophets, "in these last days he has spoken to us by a Son" (1:2). This New Testament writing marshals many quotations from and allusions to the Old Testament to encourage its original readers to remain strong in their Christian faith. Its first readers seem to have been mainly Jews who adopted the Christian faith but were having second thoughts about the wisdom of their decision. The author wanted to show that their traditional Scriptures pointed to and found their full meaning in Jesus. He explains his practice on the grounds that "the word of God is living and active, sharper than any two-edged sword" (4:12).

In the Catholic view, the Bible is a collection of words about the Word. Catholics believe that the key that opens up and gives coherence to the many words contained in the Bible is Jesus the Word of God. Because God has spoken to us in Jesus the Word made flesh, we can understand and appreciate the words of the Bible. In this sense Christianity is only secondarily a religion of the book. It is primarily the religion of a person, Jesus the Word of God. Only because Jesus is the Word of God can we describe Christianity as a religion of the book that we call the Bible.

Questions for Reflection and Discussion

1. In what sense is the Bible the church's book? In what ways did the Bible contribute to forming the church?
2. What are some common themes running through the modern Catholic documentation on the Bible and its interpretation? Which such theme is most important to you?
3. Have you ever experienced the Bible as "the word of God" in personal or public reading of a biblical text? Which text, and what did it mean to you?

What Is in the
Catholic Bible?

> *"Relying on the faith of the apostolic age, Holy
> Mother Church holds as sacred and canonical the
> complete books of the Old and New Testaments, with
> all their parts on the grounds that, written under
> the inspiration of the Holy Spirit, they have God as
> their author, and they have been handed on as such
> to the church herself."* (Dei verbum *11*)

I live in an area that is famous for its great institutions of
higher education (Harvard, MIT, Boston College, Boston
University, Tufts, Wellesley, etc.). There are nine graduate
schools of theology in the area, all members of the Boston
Theological Institute, a consortium in which any student at any

17

school can take any course in any other school. Where there are so many institutions of higher education, there are bound to be many great bookstores. You can spend a lot of time (profitably!) simply browsing around any one of them. If anything, there is an embarrassment of riches to be found there. This also presents some challenges. Which book should I buy?

Many of these bookstores carry a good selection of recently published Bibles in English. The challenge here is deciding which Bible to buy. This raises the prior questions: Why are there different Bibles, and what makes them different? Some of these Bibles contain only the Old Testament or only the New Testament. Others have both Testaments. And still others contain not only the two Testaments but also some additional books called the "Apocrypha." Why then are there different Bibles, and how did it get that way? Is there a Catholic Bible? What is in it?

The Different Canons

In Christian theology the word *canon* designates the list of sacred writings whose content provides the rule or norm for Christian faith and practice. As we noted earlier, the term *canon* derives from the Greek word *kanon,* which means "reed," "measuring stick," or "ruler." In the first Christian centuries the idea of *canon* as referring to the rule or norm of Christian doctrine and life predominated. But by the second half of the fourth century *canon* and its derivatives began to be applied also to the list of books judged to be sacred to Christians. How exactly this list emerged is not entirely clear on the historical level. But a major factor was the widespead use of certain books in the churches, and their acceptance and approval at meetings of local church leaders known as "synods." For example, the Synod of Laodicea in A.D. 363 decreed that only canonical books could be read in the churches. So by the late fourth century the two elements of the word *canon*—the rule or norm for Christian life, and the list of books sacred to Christians—had come together in the Bible.[1]

All Christians today accept the books of the Hebrew Bible as the first part (the "Old Testament") of their canon of Sacred Scripture. The Jewish tradition counts twenty-four books and divides them into three categories: the Torah (Genesis, Exodus, Leviticus, Numbers, Deuteronomy), the Former and Latter Prophets (Joshua, Judges, 1–2 Samuel, 1–2 Kings, Isaiah, Jeremiah, Ezekiel, Twelve Minor Prophets), and the Writings (Psalms, Job, Proverbs, Ruth, Song of Songs, Ecclesiastes, Lamentations, Esther, Daniel, Ezra-Nehemiah, 1–2 Chronicles). This collection is customarily referred to by Jews as the "Tanakh," which is an acronym derived from the first Hebrew letter of each division: *Torah* (Law), *Nebiim* (Prophets), and *Ketubim* (Writings).

The content of the Old Testament in Protestant versions of the Bible matches that of the Hebrew Bible. However, the material is arranged differently (under the influence of the Greek Bible tradition, known as the Septuagint) and is divided into thirty-nine books. The "two-volume" historical books (1 and 2 Samuel, 1 and 2 Kings, Ezra and Nehemiah, and 1 and 2 Chronicles) and each of the Twelve Minor Prophets are counted as separate books. The thirty-nine books appear in four categories: the Law (Genesis through Deuteronomy), the Historical Books (Joshua through Esther), the Wisdom Books (Job through Song of Songs), and the Prophets (Isaiah through Malachi).

Bibles published under Roman Catholic auspices include all the books in the Hebrew Bible along with seven more books—Tobit, Judith, 1 and 2 Maccabees, Wisdom, Sirach, and Baruch—and some additions to Esther and Daniel. These additional books were part of the Septuagint (Greek) Bible tradition, which was followed in general in the Vulgate (Latin) Bible tradition. In Catholic Bibles they are interspersed among the uncontested books of the Hebrew tradition, whereas the Protestant Bibles that include them print them as appendices to the Old Testament. These books are sometimes called "deuterocanonical," since their place in the canon of Scripture is regarded as "secondary" (from the Greek adjective *deuteros*) in comparison with the "protocanonical" or uncontested books in the Hebrew Bible. They are also known as the "apocryphal" ("hidden" or "secret") books. The biblical canons of various Orthodox churches include some books even over and above those that appear in the Roman Catholic Bibles.[2]

The canon of the Old Testament contained in Catholic Bibles today consists of forty-six books. They appear in four categories: the Pentateuch (Genesis, Exodus, Leviticus, Numbers, Deuteronomy), the Historical Books (Joshua, Judges, Ruth, 1 Samuel, 2 Samuel, 1 Kings, 2 Kings, 1 Chronicles, 2 Chronicles, Ezra, Nehemiah, Tobit, Judith, Esther, 1 Maccabees, 2 Maccabees), the Wisdom Books (Job, Psalms, Proverbs, Ecclesiastes, Song of Songs, Wisdom, Sirach/Ecclesiasticus), and the Prophetic Books (Isaiah, Jeremiah, Lamentations, Baruch, Ezekiel, Daniel, Hosea, Joel, Amos, Obadiah, Jonah, Micah, Nahum, Habakkuk, Zephaniah, Haggai, Zechariah, Malachi).

All Christians today follow the same canon of twenty-seven New Testament books. The first part of the New Testament consists of the four Gospels attributed to Matthew, Mark, Luke, and John, as well as the Acts of the Apostles (written by the author of Luke's Gospel). The thirteen Epistles attributed to Paul are presented in two blocks: the nine addressed to communities (Romans, 1 and 2 Corinthians, Galatians, Ephesians, Philippians, Colossians, 1 and 2 Thessalonians) and the four addressed to individuals (1 and 2 Timothy, Titus, Philemon). Within these two blocks the letters are arranged according to their length, from the longest to the shortest (but Ephesians is slightly longer than Galatians). Following the Pauline letters is the Letter to the Hebrews, probably because of its traditional connection to Paul (see 13:22–25). Hebrews is followed in turn by the seven "Catholic" or "General" Epistles: James, 1 and 2 Peter, 1, 2, and 3 John, and Jude. The last book in the New Testament is Revelation, or the Apocalypse, of John.

The History of the Old Testament Canon(s)

The process by which certain books in what Christians call the Old Testament came to be acknowledged as "canonical" is complicated and sometimes obscure. It is safe to say that by the late first century A.D. Jews were making a distinction between their sacred (or canonical) books and other writings. These twenty-four (twenty-two in one ancient source) books included the Torah, the Prophets, and the Writings (the "Tanakh").

The canonical process within Judaism may go back to the time of Ezra (fifth century B.C.), who was given a mandate by the Persian emperor that he should govern the land of Israel according to "the wisdom of your God which is in your hand" (Ezra 7:25). That expression may refer to the Torah (or something like it), the first five books of the Hebrew Scriptures that had recently been edited in Babylon and could serve as the rule or norm for Jewish life in postexilic Israel.

In the mid-second century B.C., according to 1 Maccabees 1:56–57, the enemies of the pious within Israel had copies of the Torah confiscated and destroyed, and saw to it that Jews who held onto them were punished. And according to 2 Maccabees 2:14, Judas Maccabeus, the leader of the successful Jewish rebellion, collected the books that had been lost and saw to their preservation. In the late second century B.C. the grandson of Jesus ben Sira (who wrote the book of Sirach/Ecclesiasticus in Hebrew around 180 B.C.) noted in the prologue to his Greek translation that his grandfather had devoted himself to the "reading of the law and the prophets and the other books of our fathers."

The oldest Hebrew biblical manuscripts (third or second century B.C. to the first century A.D.) have been found among the Dead Sea Scrolls discovered in the late 1940s. The Jewish (probably Essene) community that lived at Qumran by the Dead Sea studied, copied, and preserved all the books (except Esther[3])—that appear in the traditional Hebrew canon of Scripture. They often referred to these books in their own sectarian writings and clearly regarded them as somehow authoritative. However, we cannot be sure that these people had a notion of the "canon" of Sacred Scripture or that they regarded specific books as "canonical" in the later sense.

When we reach the late first century A.D., we are on firmer ground. The Jewish historian Josephus, in replying to anti-Jewish slanders from an Egyptian named Apion, contrasted the "myriads of inconsistent books" possessed by the Greeks with the twenty-two(!) books of the Hebrew Scriptures consisting of the five books of Moses, the thirteen books of the Prophets, and four other writings (*Against Apion* 1.37–43). Since there are twenty-two letters in the Hebrew alphabet, Josephus may have adjusted the counting of the Hebrew books in order to suggest that all wisdom resides in these books.

The traditional number of twenty-four books in the Hebrew Bible appears in 2 Esdras (also known as 4 Ezra) 14:45–46, a Jewish work written in the late first or early second century A.D. That passage distinguishes between the twenty-four books that are to be read in public (canonical) and seventy other books to be hidden away (apocryphal) from the general Jewish public and given only to the wise. The names of the twenty-four books are listed in an early tradition (*baraita*) in tractate *Baba Bathra* of the Babylonian Talmud. Another early rabbinic text (Mishnah *Yadayim* 3:5) states as a principle, "all the Sacred Scriptures make the hands unclean." The implication is that after touching the canonical books (usually in the form of individual scrolls) one should wash one's hands, since these books are "sacred" and therefore "dangerous."[4]

There were disputes among Jewish teachers about which books (Ecclesiastes, Song of Songs, Ezekiel, Proverbs, and Esther were controversial) belonged in Israel's Sacred Scriptures. Whether there was an official meeting of Jewish leaders in the late first century A.D. to decide the precise content of their biblical canon at the so-called Synod (or Council) of Yavneh (or Jamnia) has been rendered increasingly dubious by modern scholarship. The process of "canonizing" the Hebrew Scriptures seems to have been more fluid and complicated than that.

While Jesus and the first Christians in Palestine presumably used Hebrew versions of the Bible, as soon as Christianity moved outside the land of Israel through apostles like Paul and Barnabas who first worked in local Jewish communities spread over the Mediterranean world and then extended the

gospel to non-Jews too, the Greek Septuagint became the
Bible of the church. The Septuagint refers to the Greek translations of various Hebrew books that were produced in
Alexandria of Egypt. While intended primarily for Diaspora
Jews (those living outside the Land of Israel, and whose first
language was Greek), it also served to make Israel's Scriptures
available to interested non-Jews (like many Gentile
Christians). The process of translating the Hebrew Scriptures
into Greek may have begun as early as the third century B.C.,
and it continued with various revisions well into the second
century A.D.

When early Christians began to claim that certain
Septuagint passages (for example, the use of the Greek noun
parthenos meaning "virgin" in Isaiah 7:14) proved their
beliefs in Jesus (in this case, his virginal conception) and
established their conviction that Jesus provided the key to
interpreting the Jewish Scriptures, Jews reacted in two ways.
Some like Theodotion and Aquila set about producing "more
accurate" Greek translations, while other Jews seemed to
cede the Septuagint to the Christians and confined themselves to the Hebrew Bible and the Aramaic paraphrases of it
known as the Targums. The bulk of the textual evidence that
we now have for the Septuagint has been handed on in
Christian circles.

With respect to the canon of Scripture, what we know
with certainty is that Christians (probably under Jewish influence) included in their Greek Bible manuscripts some books
not customarily found among the twenty-four books of the
Hebrew canon. Not all the same "additional" books appear
in every Greek manuscript. Indeed there is a good deal of fluidity regarding the content of the Greek Septuagint manuscripts. However, prominent among the "additional" books

are the seven "deuterocanonical" books—Tobit, Judith, 1 and 2 Maccabees, Wisdom, Sirach, and Baruch—as well as the expanded versions of Esther and Daniel. These books also became part of the Christian Latin Bible tradition, which generally followed the Greek tradition.

In the Latin west these "additional" books were part of canonical Scripture for Christians at least from the late second century A.D. onward. However, in the late fourth century, Jerome, the most famous biblical scholar of the patristic era, suggested that the "deuterocanonical" or "apocryphal" books should not be regarded as fully canonical or be used for establishing church doctrine. Thus Jerome became the champion of "Hebrew truth," since his Old Testament canon corresponded to the one in use among Jews. But Augustine defended the wider Greek and Latin canon, and his view (which was nearly universally accepted by then) was endorsed by various church councils in the late fourth and early fifth centuries. Thus the wider canon including the disputed books remained as the church's Old Testament canon up to the Protestant Reformation in the sixteenth century.

In the sixteenth century Martin Luther, a Catholic monk whose criticisms of certain church practices and beliefs led to the Protestant Reformation, raised a doctrinal objection to the traditional Catholic use of 2 Maccabees 12:45–46 as the biblical basis for doctrines about prayers for the dead, purgatory, and indulgences. He also criticized 2 Maccabees for being too Jewish (and too Catholic) in its general theological outlook. And so he proposed an acceptance of Jerome's principle that the deuterocanonical books, though generally good and edifying in content, ought not to be considered canonical on the same level as the other Old Testament books or be used in establishing Christian doctrines. In his German translation of the Bible (1534), Luther relegated the deuterocanonical books to an appendix, and limited his Old Testament canon to those books that belonged to the Hebrew Bible ("Hebrew truth"). He was followed in this decision by most of the other Protestant Reformers.

In response to Luther's proposal the Catholic Council of Trent in 1546 reaffirmed the tradition of the wider Old Testament canon including the seven disputed books. It also promulgated for the first time a definitive list of the books that comprise the Old and New Testaments. And it declared that anyone who does not accept "as sacred and canonical these books in their entirety and with all their parts . . ., let that one be anathema" (Session 4, Decree 1). This is why Catholics and Protestants today have different canons in their versions of the Old Testament.

Does the presence of the disputed books in the Catholic (and Orthodox) canon of the Old Testament make a difference? I think that it does. And I am happy that the earlier Protestant practice (from Luther onward) of including these books, even if not acknowledged as fully canonical, has been resumed in most Bibles now published under Protestant auspices.

The books of Tobit and Judith are now recognized not as history books but rather as charming short stories, much like the canonical books of Jonah and Esther. While limited in historical data, they do supply important perspectives on postexilic (from the fifth century B.C. to the first century A.D.) Jewish piety. The First and Second Books of Maccabees do provide much solid information about Jewish life in the second century B.C., and take the narrative of Jewish history beyond what appears in the Hebrew Bible. The book of Baruch illustrates how certain biblical passages (Daniel 9, Job 28, Isaiah 40–66) were read and interpreted in new circumstances to provide insights about the meaning of Israel's exile from and return to the land.

The book of Sirach (also known as Ecclesiasticus) is the largest Jewish wisdom book from antiquity, and is remarkable for integrating ancient Near Eastern wisdom traditions with distinctively Jewish theological perspectives on creation, the Torah, and Israel's history. The book of Wisdom is especially noteworthy for blending Jewish biblical traditions with terms and concepts from Greek philosophy, and for insisting on life after death and rewards and punishments in the afterlife for one's deeds during life on earth. These books do make a difference, and I believe that Catholic (and Protestant) Bibles are richer for their presence.

The History of the New Testament Canon

The development of the New Testament canon is equally complicated and fascinating. There is no indication that the earliest Christians set out to produce a "New Testament" or their own "canon" of Sacred Scripture. The Old Testament was the Bible for the earliest Christians. But by A.D. 200 there was general acceptance in the churches of what may be regarded as the core books of what came to be the New Testament canon: the four Gospels, the Pauline epistles, 1 Peter, and 1 John. And by around A.D. 400 most of the Eastern and Western churches had embraced the twenty-seven-book New Testament canon used ever since in Christian churches.

The New Testament canonical process began most likely with Paul's letters. While these letters were originally addressed to specific Christian communities and their pastoral problems, very soon these letters were judged to have lasting value for other Christians too. And so they were collected into packets and sent around to other communities. Likewise, the four Gospels, though probably composed with the pastoral needs of particular communities in mind, soon began to be circulated and read all over the Mediterranean world. The "Scriptures" of the early churches were still the Greek version of the Old Testament. But once the Pauline letters and the Gospels came to be read in the various churches and gained some sort of religious authority, the movement toward the concept of a canonical New Testament composed of writings by Christians was launched.

The development of a New Testament canon was facilitated by two extreme forces within early Christianity. On the one hand, Marcion, a wealthy Christian living in Rome in the mid-second century, rejected the Old Testament, and proposed as Christian Scripture only Luke's Gospel and nine Pauline letters (and even these in edited versions, purged of "Jewish" elements). On the other hand, Christian "gnostics" (literally, those "in the know") and others were producing books that they called Gospels, which purported to describe revelations of Christ to New Testament figures such as Thomas, Peter, Philip, James, and Mary Magdalene.

The mainline churches at Rome and elsewhere refused to jettison the Greek Old Testament. After all, it was their Bible and the earliest source for Christian theology. But they also did not wish to expand their Bible to include all the new documents emanating from gnostic circles. There was no universally authoritative church council to decide the matter. In fact, the matter seems to have been resolved (under the Holy Spirit's guidance, from a Christian perspective) gradually and somewhat obscurely (at least to historians).

There seem to have been three main criteria at work in shaping the canon of the New Testament: orthodoxy of content, apostolic origin, and acceptance by and use in the churches. While these criteria were never announced by any authoritative body or person, they can be deduced from what happened.

The core of the Christian New Testament was already constituted by Paul's letters and the four Gospels. With regard to other books, orthodoxy meant that a book had to be consistent with the basic doctrines recognized as normative by the churches. Apostolicity suggests at least some presumption of an apostle as the author (Matthew, John, Paul, Peter, James, Jude) or some association with an apostle (Mark with Paul and Peter, Luke with Paul). Acceptance indicates that the books were being used widely in local churches and were being cited by reliable bishops and theologians.

The various lists of canonical books from both the East and the West show that by the late fourth century there was general consensus about the core of the New Testament canon and controversy regarding "marginal" books such as Hebrews, some Catholic Epistles, and Revelation. In his Easter letter of A.D. 367, Athanasius, the bishop of Alexandria in Egypt, included a list of the twenty-seven books that still make up the traditional New Testament canon: the four Gospels, Acts, the thirteen Pauline letters, Hebrews, the seven Catholic Epistles, and Revelation. He asserted that "in these alone is the teaching of true religion proclaimed as good news; let no one add to these or take anything from them."

Athanasius' statement did not command universal authority in the churches, and there were still disputes about the "marginal" books. However, the list that he gave was confirmed by Jerome and Augustine, and was approved by various local church councils in the late fourth century. So from around A.D. 400 onward the twenty-seven books in the New

Testament canon have been generally recognized as sacred and canonical writings that can and do serve as the rule or norm for Christian faith and practice.

The most serious challenge to this consensus came again with Martin Luther in the sixteenth century. Luther had theological problems with four New Testament books: Hebrews, because it taught that there is no repentance for sinners after baptism; James, because it did not adequately proclaim Christ; Jude, because it quoted noncanonical Jewish sources (*1 Enoch, Assumption of Moses*); and Revelation, because it lacked the proper prophetic and apostolic dimensions. While Luther never removed these books from his German translation of the Bible, he did place them at the end of his New Testament as his way of underlining their "marginal" character. On the other hand, Luther regarded certain other New Testament books as especially successful in proclaiming Christ: Paul's letters to the Galatians and to the Romans, John's Gospel, and 1 Peter.

In this way Luther raised the interesting theological issue of "the canon within the canon." The idea is that some biblical books have been and are more important than others. On the practical level some such choice seems inevitable. One can say legitimately that Catholics through the centuries have given disproportionate attention to Matthew's Gospel and the Pastorals (1 and 2 Timothy, Titus). But to raise "the canon within the canon" to the level of a theological principle and to ignore those books judged to be of secondary importance is to run the risk of rejecting the church's longstanding tradition regarding the canon and of depriving the church of the theological diversity within the New Testament canon.

At its fourth session (1546) the Council of Trent also listed the twenty-seven "sacred and canonical" books that constitute the New Testament in the Catholic Church. Many Protestant groups followed suit in confirming the traditional contents of the New Testament canon. Luther's stimulating challenge is taken up from time to time by historians and theologians, and still sparks lively debates. But among Christians today there is general agreement about what belongs in the New Testament canon of Scripture.

What then is in the Catholic Bible? In Catholic Bibles the Old Testament corresponds to what Christians have accepted as sacred and canonical through most of Christian history until the Protestant Reformation in the sixteenth century. The seven disputed books—Tobit, Judith, 1 and 2 Maccabees, Wisdom, Sirach, and Baruch—are integral parts of the Catholic (and Orthodox) Old Testament. Catholics and other Christians accept as canonical the twenty-seven books of the New Testament. These "sacred and canonical" books are recognized as providing the rule or norm for Christian faith and practice.

Questions for Reflection and Discussion

1. What can you expect to find in Jewish, Catholic, and Protestant Bibles, respectively? What will be the same, and what will be different? Does it make much difference?

2. From reading of any one of the seven "deuterocanonical" books in the Old Testament, what does it contribute? Do you think that it belongs in the Bible? Why or why not?

3. What is your own favorite book in the New Testament? Why?

How Do Catholics
Approach the Bible?

*"Therefore, since everything asserted by the inspired
authors or sacred writers should be regarded as
asserted by the Holy Spirit, it follows that we must
acknowledge the Books of Scripture as teaching
firmly, faithfully, and without error the truth that
God wishes to be recorded in the sacred writings for
the sake of our salvation."* (Dei verbum 11)

It has been my privilege for over thirty years to teach biblical studies at the Weston Jesuit School of Theology in
Cambridge, Massachusetts. Roughly half of our students are
Jesuits studying for ordination to the Catholic priesthood,
while the other half are a wonderful mixture of Capuchin

Franciscans, women religious, and marvelously talented lay-women and -men dedicated to ministry in the Catholic Church. It is an exciting place to teach, and no one has ever questioned the need to study Scripture.

In recent years our student body has been greatly enriched by "international" students from Africa, Asia, Australia, Latin America, and Europe. Many of them—but not all—are Jesuits doing part of their theological training at our school. I have taught courses with about thirty-five students in which fifteen different countries were represented. The discussions are wonderful, primarily because of the extra-ordinary cultural diversity in the room. However, because most of our students are Catholics, there is also a certain unity in their religious imagination and their theology. This phenomenon suggests that we can legitimately speak of a kind of Catholic theological consciousness and even a Catholic imagination.

This chapter will explore some presuppositions that our culturally diverse students bring to their study of Scripture precisely because they are Catholics. It will first discuss the nature of the Bible according to the "high" Catholic theological tradition in terms of revelation, inspiration, and inerrancy. Then it will look at some elements in the shared experience that Catholics bring to the Bible. Finally it describes the most prominent Catholic Bible translations available and in wide use today in the English-speaking world.

The Catholic Theological Tradition on the Bible

For some readers the Bible is an interesting resource for understanding history and culture in the ancient Near East and the Greco-Roman world. For others it is a literary classic, a book that has managed to transcend the circumstances of its composition and to win a place in the corpus of world literature. What kind of a book is the Bible for Catholics? While Catholics can and do (and correctly so!) regard the Bible as an important historical source and as great literature, for them it is much more.

As we saw in chapter 1, Catholics regard the Bible as "the word of God in human language." That formula seeks to hold together the transcendent character of Sacred Scripture and its human formulations. While the Bible may look like other books and may be studied profitably as other books are with the techniques of literary and historical criticism, for Catholics (and other Christians) the Bible is ultimately different because of its divine origin and nature.

Theologians have traditionally expressed the "different" character of the Bible by means of three terms: revelation, inspiration, and inerrancy.[1] These are complicated terms, with even more complicated theological histories. As a pastoral council, Vatican II used these terms without trying to adjudicate the theological disputes surrounding them. Rather, the goal in *Dei verbum* was to express the fundamental significance of these words for the ways in which the Bible should be read and interpreted within the church.

According to *Dei verbum* 2, revelation is basically God's self-revelation, or God's own self-communication to the world: "It has pleased God in his goodness and wisdom to reveal himself and to make known the mystery of his will." The Bible, of course, is not the only means of God's self-revelation. According to the Catholic theological tradition, there are several sources of divine revelation besides the Bible: creation, history, human persons, society, tradition, and reason. However, the Bible is perceived as a source where divine revelation is particularly clear, and so the Bible is considered to be a precious channel for divine revelation. It is both a witness to divine revelation and an occasion for divine revelation.

Vatican II insists on the primacy of God's personal self-revelation: "By divine revelation God has chosen to manifest himself and to communicate the eternal decrees of his salvific will" (*Dei verbum* 6). The order adopted in this sentence gives pride of place to the personal dimension of the divine self-revelation without denying the importance of its contents. Through the Bible (and the other sources of revelation) we can encounter the mystery of God, not simply theological propositions, lists of commandments, and interesting stories. God's personal self-revelation provides the meaningful context for whatever propositions, commandments, and stories there are in the Bible.

Inspiration is a classical way of talking about the divine origin of Sacred Scripture ("the word of God"). The classical New Testament text for defending the divine inspiration of Scripture appears in 2 Timothy 3:16: "All scripture is inspired by God and is useful for teaching, for reproof, for correction, and for training in righteousness." The "Scripture" referred to in this text is what Catholics call the Old Testament. The early Christians seem to have taken over from Judaism their belief in the divine inspiration of Scripture. Christians today regard their Scriptures consisting of both the Old and the New Testaments as inspired by God.

The role of the divine inspirer of Scripture has traditionally been assigned to the Holy Spirit: "The divinely revealed truths that are contained and presented in the text of Sacred Scripture have been written down under the inspiration of the Holy Spirit" (*Dei verbum* 11). The role of the human authors in the process of biblical inspiration has become more complicated through the findings of modern biblical scholarship. The older model of the Holy Spirit "dictating" to the individual human writers appears to have been a crude oversimplification. Rather, the complex historical processes by which our biblical books came to be—as illustrated by the use of various sources within the Torah, the anthological character of the prophetic and wisdom books, and the three stages in the composition of the Gospels—suggest that the divine inspiration of the Scriptures must be located more within the community life of ancient Israel and the early church than in the personal psychology of individual figures such as Moses, Isaiah, and Mark.

Inerrancy for Catholics means that the Bible is a trustworthy guide on the road to salvation. According to *Dei verbum* 11, the books of the Bible teach "firmly, faithfully, and without error the truth that God wished to be recorded in the sacred writings for the sake of our salvation." That statement expresses the doctrine of biblical inerrancy in a positive way. What is really at stake is the truthfulness or trustworthiness of the Bible. Challenges to the inerrancy of the Bible came to the fore especially from the findings of the natural sciences and from the religious skepticism of the European Enlightenment. In reaction, some church leaders sought to extend biblical inerrancy to everything contained in the Bible, including the creation account in Genesis 1.

The modern Catholic approach to biblical inerrancy is best captured in *Dei verbum*'s phrase "the truth that God wished to be recorded in the sacred writings for the sake of our salvation." Without explicitly endorsing the theological position of "limited inerrancy," Vatican II avoided the defensive strategy of trying to protect the Bible against charges of scientific and historical errors. Rather, what really counts is "our salvation," and the Bible remains a trustworthy guide to reaching that goal.

It is not enough to pick out one text like Genesis 1 and accuse all of Scripture of being erroneous. The modern Catholic approach to biblical inerrancy insists that individual texts must be read in the context of the whole canon of Scripture. Moreover, from Pope Pius XII onward, the official Catholic documents on the Bible have affirmed that biblical texts must be interpreted in light of their use of ancient literary forms and in the context of ancient Near Eastern and Greco-Roman culture. When placed alongside other ancient creation accounts, Genesis 1 emerges not as a scientific treatise but rather as a theological meditation on the sovereignty of the God of Israel over all creation, the order that God has imposed upon creation, and the place of Sabbath observance within the fabric of creation.

For Catholics the Bible is both like other books (and so should be studied from the perspectives of literary and historical criticism) and different from other books (and so should be honored as "the word of God in human language"). The Bible is a privileged witness to God's own self-revelation. Its origin is with the Holy Spirit working mysteriously but effectively among the people of God. And it provides trustworthy guidance on the road to salvation.

The Catholic Experience

One of the most fruitful developments in recent biblical scholarship has been the increased attention given to the situation and role of the reader, and what the reader brings to the biblical text. Many obvious personal factors come into play when we read a biblical text. I am a male, an American, in my mid-sixties, a professor, a Jesuit priest, with advanced training in biblical studies, and so on. A Chinese woman in her thirties with little exposure to the Bible may read the same text from a different angle, and her reading may well be more insightful than mine.

The phenomenon that I just described is at the root of Bible study in the Catholic "base communities" in parts of Latin America. In them ordinary Christians (even "peasants") gather to read the Scriptures. They engage in a process that starts from their own social and political experiences, moves to reading and reflecting on pertinent biblical texts, and tries to discover points of contact or analogies between their experiences and the Scriptures. The participants are convinced that there are indeed significant analogies between the biblical text and their lives today. The goal of their reading and reflection is to discern in the light of Scripture what God might be telling them and what they might do to improve their lives and the lives of those around them. The activity of the base communities has given rise to Latin American liberation theology. But the three-step process can be used effectively in many settings.

Likewise, feminist Catholic groups ranging from parish Bible studies to high-level academic conferences of biblical professionals often adapt this structure, with great success. They not only concentrate on the liberating dimensions of Scripture itself, but also call attention to the hitherto neglected prominence of women in biblical narratives and in early church life, and seek to expose (where necessary) the patriarchal and androcentric assumptions of large parts of the Bible.

The practice of communal Bible study and the search for analogies in the Scriptures hint at the phenomenon of the

"Catholic imagination" proposed by theologian David Tracy and sociologist Andrew Greeley. In his book entitled *The Catholic Imagination,* Greeley defines the Catholic imagination as a view of the world "in which God lurks everywhere and people respond to Him as a community."[2]

The Catholic imagination seeks and finds God in all things. It looks for God's self-revelation in the realm of nature and in artistic creations made by humans such as the great cathedrals of Europe and famous paintings. It places emphasis on analogy and metaphor as ways of catching glimpses of God's activity in the world. Whereas the dialectical (Protestant) imagination highlights the otherness and transcendence of God, the analogical (Catholic) imagination stresses the nearness and immanence of God. For example, while the analogical imagination might linger on the images of God as "shepherd" or "rock," the dialectical imagination would quickly insist that these are "only" images for divine attributes and that God is most certainly not a shepherd or a rock. The dialectical imagination is "either/or," while the analogical imagination is "both/and."

The Catholic imagination gives particular attention to sacred spaces and times, and discovers the hand of God in human love, in family and community life, in social structures and hierarchies, and even in situations of suffering and loss. It gets transmitted from generation to generation chiefly by stories and narratives told within the family and the local community.

Without ignoring the biblical roots of the dialectical imagination, one can say that large parts of the Bible are governed by the analogical imagination. Scripture is full of images and metaphors that seek to bring out various aspects of the mystery of God. It communicates largely through stories and grand narratives, and gives special prominence to sacred places (especially the Jerusalem Temple) and to the calendar of Jewish festivals. It finds God in human love (Song of Songs), in community life (the people of God), and even in suffering (the lament psalms, Job).

The analogical imagination nurtured by the Catholic tradition can be very helpful in entering into the reading and interpretation of Scripture. Greeley refers to the analogical (Catholic) imagination as the "low tradition," a sociological term for a tradition that arises "from below" or from the common people in a community, rather than being imposed "from above." He contrasts it with the "high tradition" promulgated by the official church and its theologians. However, in the "both/and" spirit of Catholicism, it is fair to say that the "high tradition" too can and does make important contributions to how Catholics read the Bible today.

According to the "high tradition" thus far set forth in this book, Catholics should approach the Bible as both forming and formed by the church, as the word of God in human language, as the rule or norm (canon) for Christian faith and practice, as a privileged way of finding God, as inspired by the Holy Spirit working in and through the people of God, as providing guidance along the way to salvation, and as the primary source for Christian spirituality. When the "high" (theological) tradition combines with the "low" (analogical, metaphorical) tradition, Catholics find themselves in a good position to understand their Sacred Scriptures and live in accord with their guidance.

Catholic Bibles Today

Which Bibles do English-speaking Catholics use today? In Catholic churches in the USA the *New American Bible* (with its revised New Testament) is by far the most commonly used text in public worship. In Great Britain and other English-speaking countries the *(New) Jerusalem Bible* is the most popular. There are also Catholic editions of the *Revised Standard Version* and the *New Revised Standard Version* that are used especially in academic settings and in Bible study groups, but also in some liturgical settings. Here I want to explain why there are different modern translations, and say something about the Bible translations that are most widely used by English-speaking Catholics today.

The "official" Bible of the Roman Catholic Church is the Latin translation known as the "Vulgate" (referring to "common people," Latin *vulgus*). In English-speaking Catholic circles the translation based on the Latin Vulgate and known as the *Douay Version* (from the place in France where it was first made by English Catholics in exile in the early sixteenth century) was dominant. With *Divino afflante Spiritu* (1943) Pope Pius XII gave both permission and encouragement for Catholic scholars to translate from the original biblical languages (Hebrew, Aramaic, and Greek). In English-speaking Protestant contexts the *King James Version* (1611) was most widely used and has exercised enormous influence on the English language itself. Even though the *King James Version* has undergone various revisions in the nineteenth and twentieth centuries, it remains in use, especially in conservative Protestant churches.

The second half of the twentieth century saw a virtual explosion of new Bible translations under Catholic, Protestant, and Jewish auspices. Three factors contributing to this development were the discovery of ancient manuscripts, changes in the English language, and the emergence of different translation philosophies.

First, the discovery of the Dead Sea Scrolls in the late 1940s and early 1950s provided new evidence for the Hebrew texts of the Old Testament books that was over a thousand years older than what was previously available. Moreover, the discovery of ancient texts in languages such as Sumerian, Akkadian, Ugaritic, Egyptian, and Aramaic invigorated the whole discipline of biblical linguistics and philology. Some bib lical words or phrases that once seemed unintelligible suddenly became clear. And from the late nineteenth century on there arose a near-universal agreement among textual specialists that the family of Greek manuscripts underlying the King James Version and other English translations did not provide the earliest and best basis for the text of the New Testament. So the new translations try to take advantage of the great progress in biblical studies.

Second, in recent years there have been important developments in the English language. The meanings of many words and idioms have changed over time, and some terms used in the seventeenth-century translations had become peculiar and even unintelligible by the twentieth century. Furthermore, the last third of the twentieth century witnessed a growing sensitivity about gender and language. The older translations routinely used *man* and *he/him* to include both males and females. That practice is fading away in most contexts in which English is now spoken, written, and read.

Third, translators have been giving new attention to the purpose and the audience for which the translation is made. In light of this attention two basic approaches to translation have been distinguished. Formal equivalence (literal) translations seek to reflect closely the wording and syntax of the original writings insofar as this is possible within the limits of good English. A dynamic equivalence translation is more concerned with conveying the sense or meaning of the original text, without being overly constrained by the original's wording and syntax. Proponents of this approach claim that it can and does produce more accurate translations in that today's readers can understand better what the original author sought to communicate.

The modern English versions, whether under Catholic, Protestant, or Jewish auspices, now reflect the critically established editions of the Hebrew and Greek manuscripts. Although individuals have produced complete translations of the whole Bible or of one Testament, the more widely used versions are team productions. These teams are often now interdenominational and interconfessional. In fact, *Dei verbum* 22 envisioned and encouraged such ecumenical cooperation in the production and distribution of Bibles. The first drafts typically are prepared by biblical scholars, and are then subjected to an elaborate editorial process with regard to their accuracy and their English style. Many editions of the modern translations provide extensive introductions and notes that explain textual or linguistic problems and provide necessary historical and literary information. Then the sponsoring body cares for the final production and circulation of the translation.

The *New American Bible* (NAB) is the Bible now most commonly used in Roman Catholic churches in the United States. Rooted in a project begun in the mid-1930s under what was called the Confraternity of Catholic Doctrine (CCD), the first complete editions of the NAB comprising both Testaments appeared in 1970. The NAB was prepared by members of the Catholic Biblical Association of America, and enlisted the collaboration of several prominent Protestant scholars. The translators worked directly from the standard Hebrew and Greek editions, not from the Latin Vulgate.

The NAB sought to be suitable for public worship, private reading, and study. Its translation philosophy tended toward dynamic equivalence. Indeed, complaints about its freedom in some passages led to a full-scale revision of the New Testament that appeared in 1986. A revision of the Old Testament books is in the final stages of preparation. The revisions generally use gender-inclusive language in referring to humans where this makes sense, but leaves the masculine pronouns used for God in the Hebrew and Greek originals. The various editions of the NAB come with reliable introductions and notes that facilitate the reading of Scriptures by people at various levels of biblical expertise.

The *Jerusalem Bible* was one of several translations of the Bible made on the basis of the French *La Bible de Jérusalem* (1956). The French original was in large part the work of professors at the Ecole Biblique de Jérusalem, a school for advanced biblical and archaeological research founded by the Dominican Fathers more than a hundred years ago. Their work in introducing, translating, and annotating all the books of the Bible was the first fruit of remarkably positive and constructive developments in French Catholic biblical scholarship after World War II. A thorough revision appeared in 1973.

The English *Jerusalem Bible* was based on the original biblical languages. But in matters of exegetical controversy or dispute, it generally followed the decisions of the French translators. Moreover, it adopted and adapted the introductions and notes found in the French edition. Produced mainly by Catholic biblical scholars and literary figures in the United Kingdom (including J. R. R. Tolkein), the English *Jerusalem Bible* first appeared in 1966.

The translation philosophy adopted in the *Jerusalem Bible* went even further in the direction of dynamic equivalence than the NAB did. Some dissatisfaction with this policy led in part to the revised edition known as the *New Jerusalem Bible* (NJB) in 1985. This new edition also incorporated the improvements made in the 1973 edition of *La Bible de Jérusalem*. The revision is generally gender inclusive when speaking about human beings. While very effective for personal reading and worship, the JB was less suited for serious Bible study (because its translation was often too free). The NJB marked an improvement in this area.

The *Revised Standard Version* (RSV, 1946; second edition, 1971) was an authorized revision of the *American Standard Version* (1901), which was in turn a revision of the *King James Version* (1611). It was intended as a "traditional" version that sought to preserve the best features in the English Bible tradition. Produced under Protestant auspices, in 1965 it was granted a Catholic *imprimatur* by Cardinal Richard J. Cushing of Boston. While used in worship and private reading, the RSV was especially suited for serious study since it reflected quite well the vocabulary and sentence structure of the Hebrew and Greek originals. The RSV is still available, and many professors recommend it to their students.

Published in 1989, the *New Revised Standard Version* (NRSV) represented a thorough revision of the RSV. Several factors led to the publication of the new edition: the desire to incorporate recent discoveries such as the Dead Sea Scrolls, advances in linguistics and translation theory, and the demand for more contemporary English. The NRSV translators dealt with the gender problem by using inclusive language regarding humans where appropriate, while leaving some male pronouns referring to God.

The NRSV project enlisted the active participation of several distinguished Catholic biblical scholars. The various editions of the NRSV include the Old Testament "Apocrypha" between the Old and New Testaments, along with several other works regarded as canonical in Orthodox churches. There are even editions of the NRSV in which the books appear in the traditional Catholic order. Several publishers have produced elaborate "study Bibles" with extensive introductions and commentaries. In these projects Catholic biblical scholars have been prominent as editors and contributors.[3]

While produced under the auspices of the (Protestant) National Council of Churches, the NRSV has tried from the beginning to be an ecumenical Bible. It seeks to be suitable for public worship, private reading, and serious study. But some readers complain that its inclusive language policy sometimes distorts the meaning of the biblical texts. There will surely be further revisions. In any case, the NRSV is the most widely circulated version of the Bible in English. You can find it in most bookstores. For that reason I have used it in this book when quoting biblical texts.

Questions for Reflection and Discussion

1. In your reading of the Bible do you ever think of it in terms of revelation, inspiration, and inerrancy? What do these words mean to you?
2. Does the concept of the "analogical imagination" correspond at all to your religious experience? Does it help you in reading the Bible?
3. What kind of Bible do you have? Why did you choose that one? What features do you find to be most helpful?

How Do Catholics
Analyze a Biblical Text?

*"Now since in Sacred Scripture God has spoken
through human agents and in human fashion, the
interpreter of Sacred Scripture, in order to ascertain
what God himself wished to communicate to us,
should carefully search out what the sacred writers
truly intended to express and what God thought well
to manifest by their words."* (Dei verbum *12*)

According to the Pontifical Biblical Commission's document on "The Interpretation of the Bible in the
Church" (1993), the "historical-critical method is the indispensable method for the scientific study of the meaning of
ancient texts" (I.A). Since Catholics regard the Bible as the

word of God in human language, it follows that in studying their canonical Scriptures and the sources behind them they ought to apply the proven methods of literary and historical analysis that constitute the historical-critical method.[1]

At this point the words *critical* and *analysis* may need some explanation. For many people *critical* can sound negative and even destructive. Someone who is always finding fault and complaining is often described as *critical*. In our context, however, the term is meant to be neutral, and to refer to applying the powers of human reasoning and judging to the analysis of a literary text. If we are willing to use those tools on other works of literature, how much more should we use them on the word of God in human language!

The word *analysis* conveys to most of us an objective and even scientific connotation. However, the Greek root of the word carries an overtone of pulling something apart and focusing on the pieces. In an attempt at illustrating the historical-critical method in this chapter, we will pull apart a specific New Testament text, Matthew 11:25–30. Yet the goal of the analysis is to highlight the richness of this text on the literary, historical, and theological levels. The hope is that the reader may put the text back together and see it in all its splendor as the word of God in human language.

This is how the *New Revised Standard Version* renders Matthew 11:25–30:

> 25. At that time Jesus said, "I thank you, Father, Lord of heaven and earth, because you have hidden these things from the wise and intelligent and have revealed them to infants; 26. yes, Father, for such was your gracious will. 27. All things have been handed over to me by my Father, and no one knows the Son except the Father, and no one knows the Father except the Son and anyone to whom

the Son chooses to reveal him. 28. Come to me, all you who are weary and are carrying heavy burdens, and I will give you rest. 29. Take my yoke upon you, and learn from me; for I am gentle and humble in heart, and you will find rest for your souls. 30. For my yoke is easy, and my burden is light."

Before diving into this text, I must make one more preliminary observation on the historical-critical method. The early applications of this approach to Scripture in the nineteenth and early twentieth centuries were often undertaken by religious skeptics and rationalists who sought to reduce the Bible to the level of other books. Many of its first practitioners were enemies of the established churches and especially of the Catholic Church. While assuming the stance of objective historians, they were anything but disinterested observers. Indeed many wished to "rescue" Jesus from the church and its traditions.

But as the Pontifical Biblical Commission has insisted, it is not necessary to equate the historical-critical method and the skeptical presuppositions of its early practitioners. What follows in this chapter is a Catholic version of the historical-critical method in accord with Vatican II's *Dei verbum* and the directives of the Pontifical Biblical Commission.[2]

This approach acknowledges and celebrates the fact that Catholics regard a biblical text not merely as a literary object or as a source for ancient history but also and especially as a religious text, indeed the word of God in human language. Moreover, for Catholics, the interpretation of a biblical text does not end with its literary and historical analysis. Rather, the process of interpretation moves on to questions of the text's significance today for theology, spirituality, and church life. Taken in this context, the "historical-critical method is the indispensable method for the scientific study of the meaning" of biblical texts.

Literary Methods

Since the Bible is made up of literary texts, it is both appropriate and necessary to apply to these texts the basic concerns of literary analysis. These are the procedures that we learned in school when we were asked to analyze a poem or a short story. At its simplest and most important level, the literary analysis of a text treats its context, words and images, characters, structure, literary form, content, and function. These will be the topics in our literary analysis of Matthew 11:25–30, cited above. However, they can apply (with some adaptation) to any biblical text.[3]

1. Context. Matthew 11:25–30 appears in a part of Matthew's Gospel (chapters 11–12) that is especially concerned with the unbelief and rejection that Jesus met from many in Israel. After drawing parallels with the rejection that John the Baptist had met (11:2–19), the passage presents a series of woes and warnings against unrepentant cities in Galilee (11:20–24). Then it treats two controversies with Pharisees about Sabbath observance (12:1–14), offers a reflection on Jesus as the Suffering Servant (12:15–21), and so on. The rejections that Jesus encounters primarily concern doubts about who he really is and whether his teachings can be trusted as coming from God. In its present context, Matthew 11:25–30 seeks to explain why Jesus' wise teachings should be accepted as coming from God and why some people have rejected him.

2. Words and Images. There are no serious textual problems in the ancient Greek manuscripts and the other ancient versions of Matthew 11:25–30. Among the translations the most

serious divergence comes in translating Jesus' very first word: "I thank you" (NRSV); "I give praise to you" (NAB Revised); and "I bless you" (NJB). All three renderings are defensible. But some important texts discovered among the Dead Sea Scrolls suggest that "I thank you" may be the best translation (see the discussion in the next major section of this chapter).

Our text is rich in its terminology and imagery. In 11:25 Jesus addresses God as both "Father" and "Lord of heaven and earth," thus capturing both the intimacy of his personal relationship with God and the sovereignty that God enjoys over all creation. Then there is a set of oppositions: hidden versus revealed, and the wise and intelligent versus infants. In 11:26 this paradoxical state of affairs in which the wise fail to understand and the unlearned do understand is attributed to God's will and grace. Throughout the Bible from Genesis on, God generally uses the most unlikely instruments to achieve his purposes.

In 11:27 the Father and the Son form another pair. But here there is perfect harmony between the members. The words are used in an absolute sense: *the* Father and *the* Son. They suggest that Jesus, who calls God his "Father," has a dignity beyond all humans and such a special relationship with God that it reaches the level of divine sonship. Another pair is formed by the words "know" and "reveal." The text affirms that the knowledge or wisdom that Jesus conveys has been revealed to him by God, and that he now reveals it to humans. The supreme wisdom is revelation from God, and this is what Jesus the Son provides.

The words and images that make up Jesus' invitation in 11:28–30 appear in a "concentric" pattern. In these "concentric" structures the main point is at the center, and the elements on either side serve to highlight what appears in the middle of the text. This device is common in both Testaments and in ancient literature in general. The small unit in 11:28–30 is structured concentrically: A—burdens (11:28a); B—rest (11:28b); C—Jesus the wise teacher (11:29a); B—rest (11:29b); A—burdens (11:30). The intricate structure serves to highlight what Jesus the teacher can bring to weary and burdened persons. It also identifies Jesus as a "gentle and humble" teacher. The image of the "yoke" refers to the harness put on the shoulders of beasts of burden that pulled plows or powered mills in first-century Palestine. In ancient Jewish literature the image of the yoke was used metaphorically to refer to the challenging process of learning traditional wisdom and even to the Torah and to the kingdom of heaven. The paradox here is that Jesus' yoke is easy and his burden is light.

3. Characters. The main character is Jesus. He is the speaker throughout the text. In 11:25–26 he addresses God as "Father" and speaks about the "wise" and the "infants." In 11:27 Jesus talks about God as "my Father" and about himself as "the Son" and those to whom God wishes Jesus to reveal his wisdom. In 11:28–30 Jesus offers an invitation to those who feel weary and overburdened, and so seek for rest. In each unit Jesus is both the speaker and the central figure. But in each unit there is also reference to those who need and receive his revelation: the "infants," those to whom the Son reveals the Father, and those who seek rest.

4. Structure. There are clearly three small units: 11:25–26; 11:27; and 11:28–30. They also fit together in a kind of "concentric" structure: A—the recipients of Jesus' revelation (11:25–26); B—Jesus as the privileged revealer of God (11:27); and A—the recipients of Jesus' revelation (11:28–30). In this unit the structure helps to bring home the main point that Jesus' wisdom is from God, and he can give divine wisdom to humans.

5. Literary Forms. The literary forms by which the Matthean Jesus communicates his message in 11:25–30 are

familiar from other parts of the Bible: In the "thanksgiving" (11:25–26) Jesus addresses God and gives the reason why he is thanking God. In the "declaration" (11:27) Jesus asserts his close relationship to God in terms of the Father and the Son. And in the "invitation" (11:28–30) Jesus summons those in search of rest to come to his wisdom school.

6. Content. In its context Matthew 11:25–30 affirms that as the Son Jesus can be trusted not only as a wise teacher but also as the definitive revealer of his Father. Those who reject him and his teaching fail to understand him and the origins of his wisdom. Indeed through Jesus, God has turned human society upside down, since the "infants" understand and the teacher is "gentle and humble." In the face of the "Lord of heaven and earth," human wisdom is limited and inadequate. Jesus, however, is the privileged and definitive revealer of divine wisdom.

7. Function. In Matthew's Gospel as a whole Jesus appears as a wise teacher. This Gospel provides large samples of Jesus' wisdom in five great speeches: the Sermon on the Mount (chaps. 5–7), the Missionary Discourse (10), the Parables (13), the Community Discourse (18), and the Eschatological Discourse (24–25). Yet despite the obvious wisdom of his teaching, Jesus often finds himself rejected and in the end suffers a cruel death on the cross. Jesus' proclamation in 11:25–30 functions as a beacon of light in the midst of much darkness (which is especially emphasized in chapters 11–12). Indeed Jesus' declaration in 11:27 can be regarded as one of the central theological affirmations of the entire Gospel of Matthew.

Historical Methods

Our literary analysis of Matthew 11:25–30 has taken the text as it now stands and explored the various elements within it in the hope of better understanding how they contribute to communicating the message of the text. This kind of study is sometimes described as "synchronic" ("at the same time") analysis because it concerns the text in its final or present form, without much regard for the historical processes behind it.

The explicitly historical study of a text is called "diachronic" ("through time"). It focuses on the history of a text, especially the historical setting in which it arose and the sources used in composing the text. The historian (from the Greek root meaning "seek out, inquire") is a kind of detective, not satisfied with surface appearances but always seeking to go behind the text and find out "what really happened" and how a text came to be. The historian's task involves many areas of research, and there are several ways in which biblical scholars function as historians. Here we will look at two approaches that have been especially fruitful in modern biblical scholarship: the search for parallels and backgrounds (what was "in the air"), and tracing the history of a text.

1. Parallels and Backgrounds. In many respects Matthew's Gospel is the "most Jewish" among the four Gospels. It begins with a genealogy that traces Jesus' lineage from Abraham and David, and develops the narrative of Jesus against the background of many Old Testament quotations that contribute to Matthew's master theme of Jesus as the fulfillment of God's promises to Israel. It stands to reason then that the best place to look for pertinent parallels and background material is in early Jewish sources.

Here we will focus on three topics: the introductory formula, "I thank you," in 11:25–26, the possible Wisdom background of 11:27, and the invitation to Jesus' school in 11:28–30. In each case our concern is how Jewish parallels and backgrounds illumine the text of Matthew 11:25–30.

Example #1. The introductory formula, "I thank you," in 11:25 is capable of several translations as we have seen: "I thank," "I praise," and "I bless." One reason why I find "I thank" preferable is that its use has been greatly illumined by the discovery among the Dead Sea Scrolls of the *Hodayot* or *Thanksgiving Hymns*.[4] Developed from models found in the Old Testament book of Psalms, these texts offer thanks to God mainly for rescues from danger and for revealing knowledge about the mysteries associated with God's plan for creation. Each hymn begins with the formula, "I thank you, my God," and then gives reasons for the thanksgiving: "for you [God] have revealed yourself to me as perfect light" and "through me you [God] have illumined the face of the congregation." The speaker seems to be the Teacher of Righteousness, a great leader in the early stages (second century B.C.) of the Jewish Essene movement at Qumran.

These parallels help to clarify the meaning of the introductory formula in Matthew 11:25 and to place the passage in the context of the biblical understanding of thanksgiving. In the biblical tradition to "give thanks" is to stand up in public and point to God as the real agent in one's rescue from danger or in one's intellectual-spiritual enlightenment. In Matthew 11:25–30 Jesus uses a familiar Jewish formula to point to his heavenly Father (the Lord of heaven and earth) as the revealer of divine wisdom and to assert that as God's Son he can reveal the wisdom that comes from divine revelation.

Example #2. Jesus' declaration in Matthew 11:27 about his Father-Son relationship with God represents a remarkably high estimate of his person. Indeed it sounds more like the kind of statements that appear frequently in John's Gospel than anything in the other three Gospels. In some Jewish contexts such a statement would constitute blasphemy. However, several Jewish texts that describe Wisdom as a personal figure at least supply some illuminating Jewish background material for Jesus' extraordinary claims in Matthew 11:27.

In Proverbs 8, Wisdom appears as a female figure who claims to have been present before God created anything else (8:22) and purports to have been God's assistant in the work of creation: "Then I was beside him, like a master worker" (8:30). In Sirach 24 Wisdom sings her own praises, and claims to have been commanded by God to make her dwelling on Mount Zion at the Jerusalem Temple and to take "root in an honored people, in the portion of the Lord, his heritage" (24:12). In Wisdom 7, Wisdom is said to hold the world together as a kind of world soul. She is described as "a breath of the power of God and a pure emanation of the glory of the Almighty . . . a reflection of eternal light, a spotless mirror of the working of God, and an image of his goodness" (7:25–26). What is common to all these texts is the idea that the figure of Wisdom is intimately related to God and acts as God's intermediary and revealer in the world.

Early Christians soon made connections between Wisdom and Jesus. In a very early hymn preserved in Colossians 1:15–20, Jesus is celebrated as "the image of the invisible God, the firstborn of all creation" (compare Wisdom 7:25–26 and Proverbs 8:22). And the prologue to John's Gospel (1:1–18) affirms that "in the beginning was the Word . . . and the Word became flesh and lived among us" (compare Proverbs 8:30 and Sirach 24:12).

There are, of course, clear differences between the Jewish Wisdom texts and what early Christians believed about Jesus. In the Jewish texts Wisdom is a creature of God, whereas in Matthew 11:27 and other New Testament texts Jesus has an even higher status as the Son of God. Nevertheless, the idea of Wisdom existing before all other creatures and serving as God's agent of revelation to the world surely made it possible for Christians, even those of Jewish background, to accept and affirm statements about Jesus' divine sonship such as we find in Matthew 11:27.

Example # 3. In Matthew 11:28–30 Jesus issues an invitation to come to his school of wisdom, take up his "yoke," and find rest. The author of the book of Sirach (also known as Ecclesiasticus) was a Jewish wisdom teacher who conducted a school for aspiring scribes in Jerusalem in the early second century B.C. In an autobiographical poem at the end of his book (51:13–30), Ben Sira issues a similar invitation to prospective students: "Draw near to me, you who are uneducated, and lodge in the house of instruction" (51:23). He warns the recruits that they will need to accept the harsh discipline that the search for wisdom requires, and so he uses the image of the yoke: "Put your neck under her [Wisdom's] yoke, and let your souls receive instruction" (51:26). And he promises the same results that he himself experienced in his search for wisdom: "See with your own eyes that I have labored but little and found for myself much serenity" (51:27). The invitation, the image of the yoke, the appeal to the teacher himself, and the promise of rest all appear in Jesus' invitation to his school in Matthew 11:28–30.

We have seen three examples in which reference to ancient Jewish texts illumines various elements in Matthew 11:25–30. These texts at the very least provide parallels to what appears in the Matthean passage. Whether Jesus or Matthew was directly influenced by any one of these specific texts in formulating the New Testament passage cannot be proved or disproved. But the Jewish texts do show what was "in the air" and can help in understanding the historical context for some very important words, images, and ideas in Matthew 11:25–30.

2. The History of a Gospel Text. In the first chapter I noted that Vatican II's *Dei verbum* took over and made part

of official Catholic teaching the concept that Gospel texts must be read at three levels, corresponding to the process of development that these texts passed through in their history. The three stages are Jesus, the early church, and the Evangelist. Attention to Matthew 11:25-30 provides a good illustration of this process.

Stage 1—Jesus. The Gospels present Jesus as a Jewish wisdom teacher. That description does not exhaust his identity, of course. But even the most skeptical biblical critics agree that Jesus was at least a Jewish wisdom teacher. During his earthly ministry (as the Gospels attest) Jesus used the literary forms typically employed by Jewish wisdom teachers: proverbs, instructions, admonitions, prohibitions, parables, questions, and beatitudes. His teachings concerned many topics usually treated by Jewish wisdom teachers: marriage and family obligations, money and material goods, social relations, happiness, and relating to God. The presentation of Jesus as a Jewish wisdom teacher in Matthew 11:28–30 fits well with everything we know about the earthly Jesus.

Stage 2—The Early Church. For early Christians, however, Jesus was much more than a typical Jewish wisdom teacher. Among the other titles (Son of Man, Son of God, Messiah, Lord, etc.), they celebrated Jesus as the Wisdom of God (see Colossians 1:15–20; Hebrews 1:3), and as the Word of God made flesh (see John 1:1, 14).

As we have seen in the literary analysis, Matthew 11:25–30 consists of three short units. The first two— Matthew 11:25–26 and 11:27—appear together in Luke 10:21–22, but neither occurs in Mark's Gospel. Sayings that occur in both Matthew and Luke but not in Mark are generally regarded as having once belonged to the Sayings Source Q. The source is so named from the first letter in the German word for "source" (*Quelle*). It is considered to have been a collection of short sayings attributed to Jesus, in an anthological form something like the book of Proverbs. According to the Two-Source Theory of Synoptic Gospel relationships, both Matthew and Luke used Q independently to produce their revised and expanded versions of Mark's Gospel around A.D. 85 or 90.

I noted before the links between Matthew 11:27 with John's Gospel. There are good parallels for Matthew 11:27 in John 1:18, 3:35, 10:15, 13:3, and 17:2. These parallels probably reflect common traditions circulating in various early Christian circles rather than direct dependence of one Evangelist on another.

The invitation in Matthew 11:28–30 has no parallel in other Gospel texts. However, it does have about it the ring of tradition and may well reflect the words of Jesus the Jewish wisdom teacher. The traditional material found only in Matthew's Gospel is designated by the letter M (for Matthean).

By now the reader may have become dizzy with so many traditions—wisdom hymns, Mark, Q, John, and M. But these putative sources isolated by source criticism indicate that the period between Jesus' earthly ministry and the final composition of the four Gospels (from A.D. 30 to 70) was a lively and varied phase in which many traditions from and about Jesus were circulating in the churches.

Stage 3—The Evangelist. From the above analysis it appears that the Evangelist Matthew used two sayings already joined in Q (11:25–26, 27) and another saying from his special tradition M (11:28–30). His reason for putting all these units together seems to have been their common theme of revelation: Jesus as the revealer, and the recipients of his revelation. Matthew then placed his new unit in the middle of a section (chapters 11–12) largely devoted to the rejection of Jesus and his message. Against this gloomy background Jesus' declaration of himself as the Son of God and as the revealer to those who are open to him and seek for rest shines brightly. What Matthew did with his sources is known as his "redaction"—a term that describes the shaping, editing, and placing of traditional materials by the Evangelist for his own distinctive theological purposes.

There is also a historical dimension to redaction criticism. It is generally acknowledged that Matthew composed his Gospel around A.D. 85 or 90, against the background of an intense struggle within Judaism about the ongoing identity of Israel as the people of God. In A.D. 70 Jerusalem and its temple had been destroyed by the Romans, and Roman political control over the land of Israel had increased dramatically. Of the three major pillars of Judaism—the temple, the land, and the Law—only the Law remained in Jewish control. Some Jews (Zealots) wanted to continue the rebellion and managed to revive it under Bar Kokhba in A.D. 132–35. Other Jews (apocalyptists) looked for divine rescue in the future and counseled strict observance of the Law in the present. Still other Jews (early rabbis) gave themselves to ever more careful study of the Law and the traditions associated with it.

In this contest for the heritage of Israel, Christian Jews like Matthew and most of his community, perhaps at Antioch in Syria, contended that the Jewish tradition is best preserved and carried on among those who take Jesus of Nazareth as the authoritative representative and interpreter of that tradition. There are traces of this contest in Matthew's Gospel, especially in the polemical passages in which the "scribes and Pharisees" are sharply criticized (see especially Matthew 23).

With a text like Matthew 11:25–30, the Evangelist was making his case for Jesus as the wisest and best interpreter of the Jewish tradition. Jesus is authoritative because of his identity as the Son of God. For those with open minds (like "infants") and who seek "rest," the teaching and example of Jesus provided the answer to the search for the best way to carry on the Jewish heritage in the late first century

Theological Methods

What we have done so far in this chapter illustrates the process of literary (synchronic) and historical (diachronic) analysis of a biblical text. But Catholic biblical study also involves theological analysis. It cannot rest satisfied with the aesthetic appreciation of a text or with tracing the history behind the text. It also asks, Does this text have significance beyond the first century? What might it say to people today? These questions will be treated on a more practical level when we reach the topic of the "actualization" of Scripture. At this point we will concentrate on "biblical theology."

Biblical theology is concerned with the theological thoughts and contributions of biblical texts and their ongoing significance. It presupposes and builds upon literary and historical analysis. One simple and obvious way to start is to do biblical theology through the analysis of a specific biblical text such as Matthew 11:25–30.

Of the many themes in Matthew 11:25–30, I will list five here. First, thanksgiving in the biblical sense means pointing to God and confessing publicly what God has done in our life. Second, in the Scriptures God usually acts through the most unpromising agents, like "infants." Third, Jesus is not only a wisdom teacher but also the Wisdom of God. His relationship to God is so close that he is *the* Son to *the* Father. Fourth, true knowledge comes from the divine wisdom mediated through Jesus. Fifth, those who are weary and burdened will find rest in Jesus the gentle and humble teacher.

Any of these themes could be a fine starting point for further research in biblical theology. For example, one could trace the theme of Jesus as Wisdom throughout Matthew's Gospel, to see where it is treated elsewhere and how it fits within the Evangelist's theology as a whole. Or one could examine where the theme fits within the Gospels or the entire New Testament. One could go on to situate the theme in the context of the whole biblical canon (both Testaments). And finally since *Dei verbum* 24 describes the study of Scripture as "the soul of sacred theology," the results of a biblical-theological investigation might serve as the starting point for work in other theological disciplines.

Questions for Reflection and Discussion

1. On the basis of a careful reading of the Lord's Prayer according to Matthew 6:9–13, can you identify its key words and images, characters, structure, and literary form?

2. On the basis of a careful reading of the Lord's Prayer according to Luke 11:2–4, can you identify what is the same and what is different in comparison with Matthew 6:9–13? Why do you think there are two versions?

3. What are the most important theological themes in the Lord's Prayer? What might they tell us about Jesus' own theological vision?

How Do Catholics Read the Old Testament?

"Now the economy of salvation, foretold, recounted, and explained by the sacred authors, comes forth as the Word of God. Therefore these divinely inspired books retain lasting value" (Dei verbum 14).

What's in a name? What Jews refer to as "Tanakh" or "the Bible" is what Christians have traditionally called the "Old Testament." The Christian Bible consists of the Old Testament and the New Testament. In recent years, however, there have been objections from both Christians and Jews to "Old Testament" on the grounds that it disparages the book and reflects the Christian theology of "supersessionism" (or the replacement of Israel as God's people by the church), which is at least suggested in 2 Corinthians 3 and Hebrews.

There have been several proposals to rename the "Old Testament," and these have made their way into academic and even ecclesiastical discourse. The three most prominent replacements are the Hebrew Bible, the Jewish Scriptures, and the First Testament.

Part of the problem is rooted in our modern concepts of "old" and "new." For many of us (formed by the modern consumer culture) "old" is bad and should be thrown out, while "new" is good. But in antiquity new movements, and especially new religions and philosophies, had to show that they were really "old" and therefore "good."

Moreover, these proposals tend to cause more problems than they solve. The term "Hebrew Bible," for example, is usually paired with the "Greek Bible" for the New Testament. But the "Hebrew Bible" contains several chapters in Aramaic in the books of Ezra and Daniel. And of course, Catholic and Orthodox Christian Bibles include some books (the deuterocanonicals) that were either composed in Greek or translated into Greek. The term "Jewish Scriptures" is often linked with "Christian Scriptures." But if "Christian Scriptures" refers only to the New Testament, that expression could suggest that the Old Testament is not part of the Christian Bible. And "First Testament" seems like only a bland version of "Old Testament."

The best solution may be the practical proposal made by the famous Jewish scholar Jacob Neusner who says that Jews should speak of Tanakh or the Bible, and Christians may continue with "Old Testament" because in their respective religious traditions this is what the book has been and still is. They should respect each other's traditions, without necessarily being forced to adopt them.

Catholics generally use "Old Testament" to describe the first and largest part of their Bible. Indeed, even without the deuterocanonical books included, the Old Testament is four times bigger than the New Testament. The Old Testament is an integral part of the Catholic Bible.[1] Passages from it are read at almost all Catholic worship services. According to *Dei verbum* 14, "these divinely inspired books retain lasting value."

In this chapter I first want to describe how the Old Testament is studied today by Catholics and others according to the principles of historical criticism, and to reflect on what lasting humanistic and theological values the Old Testament displays. Then I will discuss how the books of the Old Testament were treated by Jews in Jesus' time as a way of grasping how the early Christians approached them. Finally I will sketch how Christians have read the Old Testament throughout the centuries, and address some problems that we may encounter in reading it today.

Old Testament Study Today

In most institutions of higher learning (including seminaries) the Old Testament is studied today according to the principles of historical criticism. The goal is to let the books of the Old Testament speak for themselves. One factor in the popularity of this approach over the past two centuries has been the discovery of ancient texts by archaeologists. The decipherment of these texts written in various ancient languages (Egyptian, Akkadian, Ugaritic, etc.) has revolutionized our perspectives on ancient Near Eastern culture and the world of the Old Testament. What in some cases seemed unintelligible to interpreters for thousands of years suddenly became clear in the light of the newly discovered parallel texts. Moreover, full-scale excavations in the land of Israel and all over the Near East have greatly illumined the everyday lives of the people of the Old Testament.[2]

The new discoveries have been brought to bear on specific biblical texts. And they have also contributed greatly to developing a historical approach that is concerned with situating the biblical texts in their specific time and place. This historical approach to the Old Testament was pioneered in Catholic circles by the French Dominican Fathers at the Ecole Biblique de Jerusalem. And in his pivotal encyclical on promoting biblical studies (1943) Pope Pius XII endorsed the value of linguistic, archaeological, and historical research in clarifying the meaning of the Old Testament and restoring "confidence in the authority and historical value of the Bible" (*Divino afflante Spiritu* 23).

In more recent times there has also developed a lively interest in studying the Old Testament from a literary perspective. Here specialists in literary studies from outside the biblical guild have often led the way.[3] Their studies have shown that in many cases texts in the Old Testament are carefully structured and brilliantly crafted to convey their message. Much attention has been given to the analysis of literary forms, narrative techniques, and poetic devices. Here also Catholic scholars, some based at the Pontifical Biblical Institute in Rome, have been prominent figures. The historical-critical study of the Old Testament fits well with the Catholic understanding of the Bible as "the word of God in human language."

Catholic biblical interpretation, however, does not stop with the historical and literary analysis of Old Testament texts. Rather, it moves on to the humanistic and theological dimensions of the texts. *Dei verbum* 15 provides a neat summary of what Christians can expect to find, when it says that the Old Testament books "give expression to a vivid sense of God; they contain lofty teachings about God and sound wisdom on human life, as well as a wonderful treasury of prayers; and in them the mystery of our salvation is present in a hidden way."

The Old Testament displays its vivid sense of God especially in the "call" narratives about Abraham, Moses, Isaiah, and Jeremiah. In each case God summons a person to a mission for which the person seems unqualified and/or reluctant. Nevertheless, God gives reassurance of his own continuing presence and help despite all the difficulties. Even in the great national crises throughout Israel's history, there was always the conviction that the God of Israel is the major figure, and that this God will remain faithful to his prophets and people even when they are unfaithful to God.

The God of the Old Testament is neither distant nor uninvolved in the lives of his people. Rather, the Old Testament always portrays God in relationship to his people. It does not deal in theological abstractions or speculations about the divine essence. The text in which the Old Testament comes closest to a definition of God expresses nicely its understanding of God: "The Lord, the Lord, a God merciful and gracious, slow to anger, and abounding in steadfast love and faithfulness" (Exodus 34:6). The two most prominent attributes of the God of the Old Testament are justice and mercy. These attributes are conceived not as opposites but rather as complementing one another. This is the one whom Jesus addresses both as "Father" and as "Lord of heaven and earth" in Matthew 11:25. The basic thesis of the Old Testament is that the creator and sustainer of the universe has entered into a covenantal relationship with the people of Israel and through Israel with all of humankind.

The Old Testament is clearly a grand repository of human wisdom. The Western concept of the rule of law and most law codes around the world have their foundations in the Torah of Israel. The Ten Commandments in Exodus 20 and Deuteronomy 5 remain the core of morality for Jews and Christians (and many others). The Wisdom Books distill the experience of humankind in such areas as money and financial dealings, family life, social relations, and the pursuit of justice. They offer neat and memorable summaries of that experience, and equip their readers with pithy statements that allow them to diagnose a situation and offer a clever interpretation of it.

Innocent suffering is perhaps the most challenging problem that humans encounter. And there is no more fearless and perceptive treatment of that problem than the book of Job. When Job's friends insist that he must have sinned (otherwise he would not be suffering), Job maintains his innocence and raises questions about the justice of God.

The Old Testament book of Psalms has been called both the hymnbook of the Jerusalem temple and the prayerbook of the church. One of the great achievements of modern biblical study has been the recognition of different literary forms or scripts among the 150 psalms, and an appreciation of how these psalms functioned in worship at the Jerusalem temple. The lament psalms (for example, Psalm 22) constitute a major category among the biblical psalms. In these laments a suffering person (or community) addresses God directly, describes and complains about the present sufferings, professes trust in God's power and care, asks for a resolution of the suffering, and usually ends on a note of thanksgiving. Throughout the centuries and today, the lament psalms have given suffering persons the recognition that they are not alone in their sufferings, have provided the words and concepts in which they might express their pain, and offered them the freedom to bring their suffering to God in an honest way.

The Old Testament is both a national epic and a witness to salvation history. It tells the story of Israel as the people of God from Abraham through the return from exile in Babylon and reestablishment in the land of Israel. What sets the Old Testament apart from ancient chronicles and modern history books is its concentration on God's actions on his people's behalf and on their responses to God. It features the great figures of salvation history: Abraham, Joseph, Moses, David, Elijah and Elisha, Isaiah, Jeremiah, Ezekiel, Ezra and Nehemiah, and the Maccabees. These figures have served as types or models not only for Jesus but also for many other persons throughout the centuries.

While highlighting the positive values of the Old Testament and insisting that it is an integral part of the Catholic Bible, *Dei verbum* 15 also speaks about some "incomplete and provisional" elements in it: "These books, even though they contain what is only incomplete and provisional, nevertheless demonstrate God's true way of instructing." What precisely constitutes these "incomplete and provisional" elements is not specified, though one can presume that they include the narratives about what amounts to genocide on Israel's part in Joshua, the calls for vengeance against Israel's enemies in some psalms, and the cynical musings of Qoheleth ("all is vanity"). Readers today might also protest against the Old Testament's shabby treatment of women (patriarchalism), acceptance of slavery, and obsession with the land of Israel.

The historical-critical method as it is practiced today focuses on the Old Testament texts themselves, and generally prescinds from their traditional Jewish and Christian interpretations. It examines the texts in the light of ancient Near Eastern culture and history, with the help of newly discovered texts and the results of archaeological excavations. It reads the texts with an eye toward their literary artistry and skill in communicating. It looks for the humanistic and theological values to be found in these books, offers critical judgments about their abiding significance, and helps to identify their "incomplete and provisional" elements. This approach to the Old Testament has proven successful in leading Catholics and others to appreciate better the Old Testament as an interesting and valuable book in its own right.

Biblical Interpretation in Jesus' Time

Catholics today can and do learn a great deal from the historical-critical analysis of Old Testament texts. But however fruitful this approach has been in modern biblical studies, it is not the only way to read a text, nor does it exhaust the significance of a text. While now certainly "indispensable," the historical-critical method does not help much in understanding how early Christian writers approached biblical texts and how those texts have been interpreted by Jews and Christians throughout the centuries.

Here I want to describe how some Jews in Jesus' time interpreted the texts that now constitute the Old Testament, with particular attention to some of the Dead Sea Scrolls from Qumran. Discussion of these texts will help us to grasp better how the New Testament writers and the Christian theological tradition have treated the Old Testament. It will also highlight the paschal mystery as the distinctively Christian interpretive key to reading the Old Testament.

Whether or not we can speak about the Jewish "canon" of Scripture in Jesus' time, it is clear that the texts that made their way into that canon already possessed some religious authority. This perception of authority in turn generated a large amount of interpretive activity surrounding these books. So Josephus in his mammoth *Jewish Antiquities* provided an extensive paraphrase of the Bible, and the writer known as Pseudo-Philo in his *Biblical Antiquities* used large parts of the biblical books to write his selective "history" of Israel from Adam to David. Both writers freely included traditions attached to their biblical sources, and offered explanations of some textual anomalies. What they did is sometimes called the "rewritten Bible."

In a huge corpus of treatises Philo of Alexandria used the allegorical methods of interpretation developed in Alexandria for dealing with pagan writings like Homer's *Iliad*, and tried to show the consonance between the Jewish Scriptures and Platonic philosophy. The rabbinic writings known as the Midrashim are large collections of traditional interpretations attached to biblical texts and arranged in commentary form. The early rabbis were famous for their efforts at explaining biblical texts in the light of other biblical texts, and for their intellectual subtlety in making exegetical and homiletical arguments.

The term *Dead Sea Scrolls* refers to the ancient manuscripts (second century B.C. to first century A.D.) discovered in the late 1940s and early 1950s at several sites near the Dead Sea in Israel. The most important site is Qumran, which seems to have been home to a branch of the Jewish religious movement known as the Essenes. Whether Qumran was a monastery, a retreat center, a publishing house, or something else, is still debated. The Qumran scrolls seem to represent the remains of the library that the community there had amassed and produced. It appears that community members hid their manuscripts in caves for "safekeeping" in the face of the attack by the Roman army that destroyed the site around A.D. 74. While there are a few almost completely intact manuscripts, the vast majority are fragmentary, some smaller than a postage stamp.

Nevertheless, despite the poor condition of most of the Qumran texts, scholars have been able to identify parts of every Old Testament book except Esther. These are now the oldest biblical manuscripts we have, by over a thousand years. They show that there was some fluidity in the wording of the biblical books. But on the whole the Qumran manuscripts confirm the basic accuracy and reliability of the process by which the books of the Hebrew Bible have been handed on through the centuries.

Among the Qumran scrolls there are also examples of the "rewritten Bible" such as the *Genesis Apocryphon* and adaptations of the book of Daniel. There are also *targums* (Aramaic paraphrases of the Hebrew Bible) for parts of Job and Leviticus, and anthologies of biblical quotations (testimony books) arranged according to their theological themes.

Some of the texts found at Qumran can be classified as "sectarian" in the sense that they reflect the ideology, community organization, and hopes of the Essene movement. The most important such works are the *Rule of Community,* the *War Scroll,* the *Damascus Document,* and the *Thanksgiving Hymns* or *Hodayot.* Here also the religious authority ascribed to the biblical texts is apparent not only in the direct quotations of them but also in the language and concepts used in the sectarian texts. In fact, the group behind these texts seems to have deliberately chosen to write Hebrew in a style that closely imitated the language and style of the biblical books.

Among the "sectarian" texts found at Qumran there is a category of biblical "commentaries" called the Pesharim.[4] The Hebrew word *pesher* means "solution, explanation." In these commentaries chiefly on prophetic texts and psalms the biblical text is regarded as a "mystery" (*raz*) to be "solved" (*pesher*). In many cases the "solution" to the "mystery" presented by the biblical text is found in the life and history of the Qumran community itself.

The *Pesher on Habakkuk* provides some good illustrations of the process. The statement, "the wicked encompass the righteous," in Habakkuk 1:4 is interpreted to mean this: "the wicked is the Wicked Priest, and the righteous is the Teacher of Righteousness." And the phrase, "that he who reads may read it speedily," in Habakkuk 2:2 is interpreted as a reference to "the Teacher of Righteousness, to whom God made known all the mysteries of the words of His servants the Prophets."

The "Teacher of Righteousness" was a major figure in the early stages of the Qumran community's history. He may well have been the legitimate claimant to the Jewish high priesthood in the mid-second century B.C. as opposed to the Maccabean usurper dubbed the "Wicked Priest." The main point for us is that these Jews regarded their Scriptures not as having been "fulfilled" in the time of their original composition, but found in their hero and their community's life and history centuries later the key to reading and interpreting the Scriptures in their own day.

The various uses of biblical texts in the Qumran scrolls can now help us to understand better how early Christians read and interpreted the "Old Testament." The early Christians certainly regarded these books as possessing religious authority. They may well have compiled their own anthologies of biblical quotations (testimonies). And they found in Jesus of Nazareth the "solution" (*pesher*) to the "mysteries" (*razim*) contained in the Scriptures. They believed Jesus to be the interpretive key to understanding the mysterious texts of the Old Testament.

In his own teachings Jesus occasionally quoted biblical texts and often alluded to them. What especially impressed his contemporaries, however, was the fact that Jesus usually taught on his own authority (see Mark 1:27). But for early Christians the Old Testament was their Bible and an important authority in its own right. One can imagine that their interpretive activity began as early as Good Friday evening as they made connections between what had happened to Jesus and texts like Psalm 22 (the lament of a righteous sufferer) and Isaiah 53 (the Suffering Servant). And from start to finish the New Testament books bear witness to the intensive efforts of early Christians in interpreting their "Bible" in light of the saving significance of Jesus' life, death, and resurrection (the paschal mystery).

Matthew's Gospel features many "formula quotations" that begin with phrases like "all this took place to fulfill what had been spoken by the Lord through the prophet" (1:22).

In his arguments about people of faith as the real children of
Abraham in Galatians 3 and Romans 4, Paul quotes and interprets one Old Testament text after another. The author of
Hebrews not only constructed his arguments about Jesus as
the Son of God and the Great High Priest out of biblical texts
but also provided a rationale for this kind of biblical exposition: "The word of God is living and active, sharper than any
two-edged sword" (4:12). And practically every sentence in
the book of Revelation is constructed out of biblical words
and phrases. For early Christians the Old Testament was a
book about Jesus Christ, and the paschal mystery provided
them with the interpretive key to it.

Reading the Old Testament as Catholic Christians

The first section of this chapter showed that *Dei verbum* 15
encourages Catholics to study the Old Testament on its own
literary and historical terms, and to look for its wise teachings
about God and the human condition. The same paragraph in
Dei verbum also stresses the importance of a "christocentric"
(that is, taking Jesus Christ as the center of and the key to the
Scriptures) reading of the Old Testament, an approach with
strong precedents in the New Testament. This is another case
of the Catholic principle of "both/and"—both the historical-
critical reading, and the christocentric or theological reading.

According to *Dei verbum* 15, "the economy of the Old
Testament was designed above all to prepare for the coming
of Christ." It goes on to cite Augustine's famous saying to the
effect that "God, the inspirer and author of the books of both
Testaments, has wisely arranged that the New be hidden in
the Old and the Old be made manifest in the New." These

two statements are classic formulations of the christocentric reading of the Old Testament, and they appear in almost all modern official Catholic documents about the Bible. They are based on the New Testament conviction that the paschal mystery is the interpretive key that can open up and resolve the mysteries of the Old Testament.

As we have seen, Marcion's rejection of the Old Testament as part of Christian Scripture seems to have served as the occasion for other Christians in the second century to embrace and champion the presence of the Old Testament in the Christian canon. But what to do with the Old Testament has often been a problem for Christian theologians.

The Church Fathers or patristic writers (Origen, John Chrysostom, Jerome, Augustine, etc.) took the Old Testament very seriously. Besides clarifying the meaning of the texts, they sought to make the Old Testament into a persuasive witness to their Christian faith. They did so by way of typology and allegory. In other words, they found in the great figures and events of the Old Testament "types" or prefigurements of Christ, and in the narratives of the Old Testament various features of the story of salvation in and through Christ. These interpretive methods, which were developed in pagan and Jewish circles, provided them with a rationale and a model for their christocentric reading of the Old Testament.

The Church Fathers found in the characters and institutions of the Old Testament the prefigurements or types of Christ, and justified this procedure on the basis of God's economy (or plan) of salvation moving from "shadows" (in the Old Testament) to "realities" (in the paschal mystery as this is represented in the New Testament). In allegorical interpretation, the persons, events, and objects described in the Old Testament are interpreted as representing the drama of the paschal mystery. Since the Church Fathers were convinced of the soteriological and even cosmic significance of the paschal mystery, they had good reason to seek and find it everywhere in the Old Testament.

Perhaps the most famous theologian in the Catholic tradition is Thomas Aquinas. One of his great achievements was bringing together in his *Summa Theologiae* revelation as found in Scripture and tradition, and reason as found in Aristotle's philosophy. However, Thomas was also a great interpreter of Scripture and a perceptive biblical theologian, a "master of the sacred page," who wrote learned commentaries on biblical books. One of his best-known biblical commentaries concerns the book of Job. What is especially fascinating in that commentary is watching how Thomas reads the book of Job through the lenses of Christian theology. For example, Thomas places Job's sufferings in their "proper" Christian theological perspective by contending that Job's eternal happiness with God and the salvation of his soul override any of his physical sufferings, and by insisting that the greatest imaginable suffering for humans is the loss of the beatific vision (the eternal experience of God). These theological ideas, of course, are foreign to the book of Job. But since Thomas was reading the Old Testament in the full light of the paschal mystery, he operated on the assumption that these ideas could and should be used in interpreting the Old Testament book of Job.

The presence of the Old Testament in the Christian Bible raises interesting questions in several areas today. For example, should Christian translators of the Old Testament insist on using "Son of Man" in Psalm 8 or "virgin" in Isaiah 7:14 on the basis of the christological interpretations of those texts in the New Testament (see Hebrews 2:5–9 and Matthew 1:23)? Does the new Catholic lectionary with its theological pattern of "promise and fulfillment" do justice to the Old Testament readings when they generally seem to serve mainly as "background" for the Gospel passage? Are Christians too selective in what Old Testament texts they read because of their narrow focus on Christ and the paschal mystery? I once heard a rabbi accuse (with some justification) Christians of tearing pages out of his family album.

However, the most serious theological problem associated with the Christian reading of the Old Testament today concerns the charge of supersessionism. Throughout the centuries, some Christians have assumed, suggested, and even proclaimed that Christians have replaced or superseded the Jewish people in the economy of salvation. The idea seems to be that Israel had its chance as God's chosen people and blew it, and we have taken their place.

Vatican II's *Nostra aetate* 4 took a different approach, one that recognizes the continuing significance of the Jewish people in the history or economy of salvation. In fact, the council's statement is really a paraphrase of Paul's meditation on God's plan of salvation history in Romans 9–11. It takes as its starting point Paul's image of God's people Israel as an olive tree. It insists that Jewish Christians like Paul and the first Christians provide the continuity for the life of the olive tree, and equates Gentile Christians with the wild branches grafted onto the olive tree. The counciliar statement goes on to observe that "the Jews remain very dear to God, for the sake of the patriarchs, since God does not take back the gifts he bestowed or the choice he made." The last part of that sentence alludes to Romans 11:29, which in turn alludes to Paul's list of Israel's prerogatives in salvation history in Romans 9:4–5. Thus the council affirmed Paul's conviction that non-Christian Israel remains an active participant in salvation history, and it made its own Paul's further conviction that in

God's own way and time "all Israel will be saved" (Romans 11:26).[5]

Biblical theologians since Vatican II have given much thought to the covenantal relationship existing between Jews and Christians. In *The Covenant Never Revoked*,[6] Norbert Lohfink, a distinguished Catholic Old Testament scholar, maintains that Christians and Jews are united in one covenant that is acknowledged in two different ways. Arguing against the common Christian view of two successive covenants, Lohfink contends that there is only one covenant, that the "new covenant" (see Jeremiah 31:31–34) is the same as the earlier one but is now made brilliant and radiant through Christ, and that God has never revoked the covenant with non-Christian Israel. By way of response, Lohfink calls on Christians and Jews to walk the twofold way of salvation "dramatically" by interacting and provoking one another to a divinely willed "jealousy" (see Romans 11:11, 14).

Questions for Reflection and Discussion

1. From the descriptions and applications of the historical-critical method in this and the preceding chapters, do you agree that it is "indispensable" in Catholic Old Testament study? What positive contributions might it make? What are its limitations?

2. Does the discussion of the use of Scripture in the Dead Sea Scrolls help you to understand better how early Christians interpreted the Old Testament?

3. What are some positive values and what are some problems associated with the traditional Christian (christocentric) reading of the Old Testament?

How Do Catholics Read
the New Testament?

*"In composing the four Gospels, the sacred writers
selected certain of the many traditions that had been
handed on either orally or in written form; others
they summarized or explicated with an eye to the situation of the churches. Moreover, they retained the
form and style of proclamation but always in such a
fashion that they related to us an honest and true
account of Jesus."* (Dei verbum *19*)

One of the great achievements in the aftermath of Vatican
II has been the new lectionary, or book of Scripture readings, to be used at eucharistic celebrations and on other liturgical occasions. The new lectionary is broken into three cycles of

readings—A, B, and C. The result is that since Vatican II, Catholic Sunday churchgoers are exposed to most of the New Testament every three years. The new lectionary was so impressive that many mainline Protestant churches quickly adopted it for themselves, with some adaptations. For example, Protestants generally do not include the texts from the Old Testament "Apocrypha" or deuterocanonical books. And in recent years they have tried to bring more continuity into the Old Testament selections. But on the whole, it is remarkable that on any given Sunday the same biblical texts are now proclaimed and preached in both Catholic and (many) Protestant churches.

Each year in the Sunday lectionary features a different Gospel: Matthew in Year A, Mark in Year B, and Luke in Year C. Selections from John's Gospel are read on many Sundays in Lent and the Easter season. The Old Testament readings generally are connected thematically with the Gospel passage. Most Catholic homilies focus on the Gospel passage. Every Sunday there is also a selection from a New Testament epistle or from Revelation. These texts, however, are on a separate cycle and have their own themes. As a result they are frequently neglected or forced to say things that they do not say. On several occasions, however, I have worked through the whole three-year cycle of epistle readings, giving special attention to what the church today might learn from the experiences of the early Christians.

In Catholic churches where there is daily Mass, there is a two-year lectionary cycle (Year 1 and Year 2) in which the first reading may be taken either from the Old Testament or from Acts or a New Testament epistle, while the second reading is from a Gospel. The first reading and the psalm are on a two-year cycle while the Gospel readings—from Mark, Matthew, and Luke in ordinary time, and from John in much of Lent and the Easter season—are repeated each year.

All this means that churchgoing Catholics today are exposed to enormous amounts of Scripture on a regular basis—most of the New Testament, and large chunks of the Old Testament—over the course of the years. And the lectionary readings are continuous, in the sense that they work right through books (Mark, Matthew, Luke, etc.) from start to finish. However, the exposure comes in small pieces, and so it is often hard for even the most attentive and devout Catholics to get perspective on what the Gospels and Epistles are, where they come from, what they are trying to say, and why they are important.[1]

This chapter first provides a sketch of how our four Gospels came to be within the context of early Christian life and history. Then it reflects on how each Evangelist portrays Jesus and describes what it means to follow him. Finally it notes some important things that we might learn from the Epistles and Revelation about the early church and about our own church today.

The Formation of the Gospels

The quotation from *Dei verbum* 19 at the head of this chapter is a careful and nuanced statement of how Catholics today should understand the formation of the Gospels. It affirms three basic points: The Gospels tell us the honest truth about Jesus; the traditions about Jesus circulated in the early churches in various forms; and the Evangelists consolidated these traditions into narratives that also addressed the pastoral needs of their own churches. This process took place from the time of Jesus' public activity and his death to the final years of the first century.

In doing justice to the complexity of the process, this approach to the Gospels lays less stress on the Evangelists as direct eyewitnesses to the events in Jesus' life than was done in the past. Rather, it emphasizes more the Evangelists as transmitters and interpreters of traditions from and about Jesus, and as theologians making these traditions relevant to Christians in their own times and places. This approach highlights how the early church, and not just a few individuals, shaped our four Gospels, and suggests ways in which the Gospels can shape our church today.

The Gospels allow us to develop an outline of the most prominent features in Jesus' life. He was raised in Nazareth, was baptized by John the Baptist, gathered disciples, exercised a ministry of teaching and healing in Galilee, went up to Jerusalem in A.D. 30 or so, was arrested and crucified by the Roman governor Pontius Pilate, and was said to have appeared alive again to some of his followers.[2]

The Gospels also tell us that the center of Jesus' preaching was the coming kingdom of God, and that he invited others to share his intimate relationship with God as "Father." They also portray Jesus as providing wise teachings about how to live in the present, showing special concern for "marginal" persons (the poor, lame, "sinners," etc.), proclaiming the forgiveness of sins and reconciliation with God, challenging people to love their enemies, and displaying a free attitude to traditions surrounding the Jewish Law. His proclamation of the kingship of God and its superiority even over the Jerusalem temple and the Law got him into trouble with both the Roman political officials and the Jewish religious leaders, and eventually resulted in his death on the cross.

These are the most basic points that the Gospels tell us about Jesus, and they are confirmed by all but the most skeptical historians. They constitute "an honest and true account about Jesus." The Catholic approach to Jesus and the Gospels affirms a strong continuity between Jesus, the early traditions about him, and the Gospels. At the same time, it acknowledges the richness and complexity of the process that led to the composition of the Gospels.

In the prologue to his Gospel (1:1–4), Luke says that the traditions about Jesus had been handed on by "eyewitnesses and servants of the word," that "many" had already undertaken to set down an orderly account of them, and that he wrote his own "orderly account" only after much personal research.

From analysis of the Gospel texts themselves, it appears that the traditions from and about Jesus circulated in the early churches in small units, both in discourse forms (parables, proverbs, prophetic warnings, rules, debates, etc.) and in narrative forms (healings, nature miracles, exorcisms, passion narratives, etc.). Beliefs about the significance of Jesus (Christology) focused first on his death and resurrection and the hope of his second coming, then on his public ministry, and finally on his origins and birth.[3] Early Christians did not set out to write books about Jesus. Their primary concern was with the person of Jesus, both in his earthly career and especially in his glorious risen state as "Lord."

The Gospels of Matthew, Mark, and Luke present a "common vision" (*synopsis*) of Jesus with regard to the outline of his ministry, the titles applied to him, and the wording in many passages. Some teachings and incidents appear in all three Synoptic Gospels, some are in two Gospels, and some are in only one Gospel. The common wording is so close in so many cases that it indicates a relationship of direct dependence among these three Gospels. John's Gospel represents an independent tradition, though it does have some links with the Synoptic tradition.

The most widely accepted explanation today of how the Synoptic Gospels are related is the Two Source Theory; that is, Matthew and Luke independently used both Mark's Gospel and the Sayings Source Q, plus some special traditions (designated as M and L). There are other, more complicated theories. The Sayings Source Q, which is a reconstruction based on passages found only in Matthew and Luke, was apparently a collection of Jesus' sayings in Greek form made around A.D. 50.

Despite their many similarities, the three Synoptic Gospels differ with regard to their literary structure, theological emphases, and the communities they addressed. John's Gospel differs from them in its three-year chronology for Jesus' public ministry and in its focus on Jesus as the revealer and the revelation of God (rather than the kingdom of God).

This account of the formation of the Gospels is by no means a sectarian Catholic construction, but one that is widely held in New Testament studies today. There are challenges to it, and in the future it may be revised somewhat. In any case, what is clear is the richness and complexity of the formation of the Gospels, which highlights once more the symbiotic relationship between the Bible and church from the earliest days of the Christian movement to the present.

The Gospels as Witnesses to Jesus and the Early Church

According to the quotation from *Dei verbum* 19 at the head of this chapter, the Evangelists "selected certain of the many traditions," wrote "with an eye to the situation of the churches," and "retained the form and style of proclamation." That is an accurate statement of what the individual Gospel writers did.

The word *gospel* derives from the Old English rendering of "good news," which was in turn a translation of the Greek word *euangelion*. In the Greek version of the book of Isaiah *euangelion* refers to the "good news" about Israel's liberation and return from exile in the sixth century B.C. The word was also used in proclamations about the Roman emperor Augustus. In Paul's letters *euangelion* is shorthand expression for the saving significance of Jesus' life, death, and resurrection.

Mark began his narrative about Jesus in this way: "The beginning of the good news (*euangelion*) of Jesus Christ the Son of God" (1:1). This usage led to the application of *euangelion* to the four canonical narratives about Jesus as if it were a literary genre (Gospel). These narratives give the impression of being biographies. And to a large extent they are, especially when measured against other ancient biographies, which emphasize the exemplary significance of their heroes rather than chronological accuracy. However, the four Gospels go beyond the ancient biographies in what they say about Jesus' identity (Son of God, Lord, etc.) and about his resurrection from the dead. Moreover, the Gospels were written by and for people who believed that Jesus was sent from God, that he revealed God's will for humankind, and that he was raised from the dead. The "faith" character of the Gospels does not mean that they are fictions or myths. But it does mean that they were written in the light of Easter by and for Christians who already knew how the story of Jesus came out.

The three Synoptic Gospels—Matthew, Mark, and Luke—present a "common vision" of Jesus. They tell the story of Jesus' public activity in three phases: his ministry of teaching and healing in Galilee; the journey of Jesus and his followers from northern Galilee to Jerusalem; and their arrival in Jerusalem, and Jesus' passion, death, and resurrection. His public ministry seems to take place in a single year, with one journey to Jerusalem. They all present Jesus not only as a teacher and healer, but also as the Son of Man, Son of David, Son of God, Messiah/Christ, Lord, and so on.

While the Synoptic Evangelists provide their common vision of Jesus, each of them also presents a distinctive witness to Jesus. Whereas Mark begins his account with Jesus as an adult undergoing John's baptism, Matthew and Luke supply infancy narratives that feature Jesus' Jewish roots and characters that represent all that is good in Judaism. Moreover, whereas Mark seems to have ended his story with the empty tomb at 16:8, Matthew and Luke give different narratives about appearances of the risen Jesus to some of his followers.

Mark seems to have been the first one to write a Gospel.[4] He portrays Jesus as the Suffering Messiah, the twelve disciples as generally foolish and cowardly (in strong contrast to Jesus), and Christian life as lived under the sign of the cross. His Gospel is traditionally associated with the apostle Peter and the threat of persecution facing the Christian community at Rome around A.D. 70.

Matthew's Gospel is often placed at Antioch in Syria (a large Greek-speaking city with a substantial Jewish population), around 85 or 90 A.D.[5] The main problem there seems to have been a struggle between rival Jewish religious groups competing for the right to carry on the heritage of Israel after the temple's destruction in A.D. 70. Matthew was particularly eager to show how Jesus fulfilled God's promises to Israel in the Old Testament. He upgrades the disciples to the extent that they at least have a "little faith." He views the church as the continuation of Israel as the people of God through the abiding presence of Jesus as "Emmanuel" ("God with us").

Luke, who is traditionally associated with Paul but has his own theological vision, wrote his Gospel around 85 or 90 A.D., perhaps somewhere in Greece.[6] He portrays Jesus as the prophet who stands in the line of Israel's great prophets Elijah and Elisha, as a good example who lives out his own teachings perfectly, and as a martyr who in his death bears witness to his heavenly Father. Luke finds in the figures of the infancy narratives (Elizabeth and Zechariah, Mary, Simeon and Anna) a principle of continuity with the time of Israel, and uses the Twelve Apostles to establish the continuity between the time of Jesus and the time of the church. With his second volume, known as the Acts of the Apostles, Luke extends the story beyond Jesus' death and resurrection.[7] In both volumes the Holy Spirit plays a central role. The Spirit empowers and guides Jesus through his public ministry and passion, and then directs the apostles and their coworkers in spreading the gospel "to the ends of the earth" (Acts 1:8).

John's Gospel offers a different vision of Jesus.[8] It stretches the narrative over three years and has Jesus make several trips to Jerusalem. In these matters John is probably more correct than the Synoptic Evangelists from a historical perspective. John's Gospel also features a different set of characters: Nicodemus, the Samaritan woman, the man born blind, Lazarus, and the "beloved disciple." John presents Jesus as the Word of God and focuses on his relationship as the Son of God to his heavenly Father. He stresses Jesus' dual role as the revealer and the revelation of God. This Gospel seems to have been composed in the late first century for a largely Jewish Christian community in Palestine, Syria, or Transjordan that was being forced out of the Jewish synagogue because of their beliefs about Jesus (see 9:22, 12:42, 16:2). The situation of this community was analogous to that of the Matthean community, and John's Gospel makes many harsh statements about "the Jews."

Are the Gospels anti-Jewish? That question arises from time to time, and became especially controversial in recent times with the release of Mel Gibson's film, *The Passion of the Christ*. One must admit that there are some highly negative comments about the "scribes and Pharisees" in Matthew 23, and about "the Jews" in John. However, these statements must be placed in the historical context of late first-century Judaism. The Evangelists who composed these Gospels were almost certainly of Jewish origin. And as Christian Jews they were engaged in the struggle about who was the true heir to Israel's identity as the people of God. I regard them as no more anti-Jewish than I consider Americans who make controversial political statements about other Americans to be anti-American.

Nevertheless, it is fair to say that the Gospels, when taken out of their historical context, are potentially anti-Jewish. This helps to explain the controversy surrounding Gibson's portrayal of the Jewish leaders in *The Passion of the Christ*. When non-Jews today see such negative and stereotypical figures, they may impose these images on their Jewish neighbors and coworkers, forgetting that Jesus, Mary, and the rest of Jesus' followers in the film were all Jews too.

An important reminder about the potential for anti-Jewish attitudes today comes from the following statement in Vatican II's document on the relationship of the Catholic church to other religions: "Even though the Jewish authorities and those who followed their lead pressed for the death of Christ, neither all Jews indiscriminately at that time, nor Jews today, can be charged with the crimes committed during his passion" (*Nostra aetate* 4).

The Epistles as Witnesses to Early Christian Faith and Life

The figure of Jesus stands at the head of the Christian movement as its origin and source. But it would be a mistake to suppose that that the Gospels were written first and so provide the earliest witnesses to Christian faith and life. In fact, the earliest complete documents in the New Testament are the letters by Paul. His first letter—1 Thessalonians—was written in A.D.

51, and his last great letter—Romans—was composed around A.D. 58. What is most remarkable is the sophisticated theological vocabulary and conceptuality that emerged so fast in the twenty years between Jesus' death and Paul's first letter. One scholar (Martin Hengel) has often described this phenomenon as "not a development but an explosion." Paul's letters and the other New Testament epistles offer glimpses into the impact of Jesus' life, death, and resurrection within the churches around the Greco-Roman world in the first Christian century.

What can be found out concerning early Christian faith and life in the New Testament epistles is neatly summarized in Vatican II's *Dei verbum* 20: "In these writings, by God's wise designs, those matters that concern Christ the Lord are confirmed, his authentic teaching is more fully stated, the saving power of Christ's divine work is proclaimed, the origins and marvelous growth of the Church are recounted, and her glorious consummation is foretold."

The lordship of Christ is especially prominent in two early Christian hymns embedded in Pauline epistles. In Philippians 2:6–11, in the course of appealing for humility and mutual respect within the Christian community, Paul quotes a hymn about Christ the Servant of God. The hymn first describes the humiliation that Christ took upon himself by becoming human and suffering death on the cross. Then it recounts how God exalted Christ in his resurrection and ascension so that "every tongue should confess that Jesus Christ is Lord, to the glory of the Father" (2:11). Likewise, the letter to the Colossians contains a hymn in 1:15–20 that celebrates the primacy of Christ first in the order of creation and then in the order of redemption. Here Jesus is portrayed as the wisdom of God: "the image of the invisible God, the firstborn of all creation." He is also called "the head of his body, the church . . . the beginning, the firstborn from the dead." The "lordship" of

Christ extends over all creation and is the foundation and guiding force of the church.

The authentic teaching of Christ was developed in the epistles as Christianity moved out of the land of Israel and faced new circumstances and challenges. The new movement thrived especially in the cities of the Roman Empire, where nonetheless temptations to idolatry and moral degradation were everywhere. Large parts of Paul's letters present moral guidance (*paraenesis*) for the new Christians as they struggled to cut their ties with former ways of living and to act in ways more consonant with their new identity. While Paul only rarely quotes sayings of Jesus, the goal of his moral and pastoral instruction was always to give direction that might deepen the participation of Christians in the life and death of Christ into which they had been baptized. The letter of James mentions the name of Jesus only twice (1:1, 2:1). But in advising Christians outside the land of Israel ("the twelve tribes in the Dispersion") James frequently alludes to wise teachings attributed to Jesus in the Gospels (especially in Matthew) and may even provide us with the "voice" of Jesus in some cases.

The saving power of Christ's divine work is the main topic in two of the most theologically rich documents in the New Testament: Paul's letter to the Romans, and the letter to the Hebrews.[9] In Romans Paul is especially interested in the saving effects or results (soteriology) of Jesus' life, death, and resurrection, and how we may participate in them (through faith). He carefully describes the plight of all humans, Jews and Gentiles alike, before and apart from Christ. Then he contrasts the First Adam and Christ the Second Adam, and describes how Christ overcame the powers of Sin, Death, and the Law, and made it possible for all to live "in the Spirit" as children of God like Christ. The letter to the Hebrews is an extended meditation on the early Christian confession that "Christ died for our sins." It shows how Christ provides the key to understanding the Old Testament, and how his sacrificial death did what the Old Testament sacrificial system could never achieve—bring about right relationship with God (justification).

The origins and growth of the church are major topics in the epistles, sometimes gloriously so, and at other times not so gloriously.[10] In the New Testament the letter to the Ephesians comes closest to being a treatise on the church. It roots the church firmly within the theological context of Jesus' death and resurrection, and describes the risen Christ as "the head over all things for the church, which is his body" (1:22–23). It celebrates the new humanity that Christ has brought about in the church by breaking down the barriers between Jews and Gentiles. This high theology of the church is balanced by the recognition that most of the epistles were responding to crises within the churches. For example, Paul's first letter to the Corinthians provides pastoral advice on the following problems that had arisen within the church at Corinth: factions and divisions within the church, sexual immorality, lawsuits among Christians, all kinds of marriage problems, participation in pagan rituals, disorder at church meetings and at the Lord's Supper, misunderstandings about the spiritual gifts, and doubts about the resurrection. It has been said with some accuracy that all the problems facing the church today can be found already at Corinth in the first century.

The "glorious consummation" foretold in the epistles refers to the fullness of the kingdom of God that one day will be made manifest in all creation. This is what Jesus taught us to pray for: "Thy kingdom come." While Jesus' resurrection was a preview or first installment, the fullness of God's kingdom remains in the future and in God's hands. In Romans 8, Paul reminds the early Christians that while they do "have the first fruits of the Spirit" through their baptism, they still await their adoption and the redemption of their bodies. Paul places their hope in a cosmic framework when he says that "creation awaits with eager longing for the revealing of the children of God" (8:19). The book of Revelation is a full-scale meditation on hope for the "glorious consummation."[11] Written for seven churches in western Asia Minor (modern Turkey) facing persecutions and internal disputes, it presents a series of visions aimed at encouraging young Christians to remain firm in their faith in the risen Christ and to await the final glorious triumph of Christ the Lamb of God. The book issues in the vision of the New Jerusalem, thus responding to Jesus' own prayer: "Thy will be done on earth as it is in heaven."

Questions for Reflection and Discussion

1. To what extent is the formation of the Gospels a reflection of the symbiotic relationship between the Bible and the church?
2. Why are there different portraits of Jesus in the New Testament? Why are there four Gospels instead of one? Is this a blessing or a problem?
3. What can the church of the twenty-first century learn from the church of the first century? Are the New Testament epistles a good source for answering this question? Why or why not?

How Do Catholics
Interpret Scripture?

*"Sacred Scripture must also be read and interpreted
in the light of the same Spirit by whom it was written." (Dei verbum 12)*

I once heard a distinguished Protestant biblical scholar and
archaeologist confess that he paid no attention to the biblical interpretation of the Church Fathers. His reason was,
"We know more than they did." He did have a point.
Through archaeological excavations and through the discovery of ancient texts and their decipherment, in some respects
we today may well know more about life in ancient Israel and
even about the Greco-Roman world than the Church Fathers
and the Jewish rabbis did.

However, historical facts and archaeology are not the whole story about biblical interpretation. Indeed, biblical scholars today have increasingly come to acknowledge that they stand in a great tradition of biblical interpretation. Those who study the history of biblical interpretation in any depth soon recognize and respect the intellectual powers and spiritual sensitivities of the interpreters of the past. Indeed, the task of interpreters today is to earn their place within that tradition.

Exposure to the traditional "spiritual" interpretations illustrates that the process of interpreting any text—but especially a biblical text—is complex. In this chapter we will explore some of the issues involved in what is often called biblical hermeneutics, or methods of interpretation. After looking at some important contributions made by modern philosophers regarding hermeneutics, we will show why and how the "spiritual" interpretation of biblical texts is an important and necessary dimension of the Catholic reading of the Bible. Then we will consider what has long been a controversial issue between Catholics and Protestants: the relationship between Scripture and tradition.

As with most issues pertaining to reading the Bible, the Catholic approach insists on both Scripture and tradition. The historical-critical method is correctly recognized as indispensable for analyzing and understanding what a biblical text communicated in its time and place of historical origin. But the traditional theological or spiritual reading of Scripture, rooted in the paschal mystery, is also indispensable for determining where particular texts stand within the larger context of Christian faith, and how they might illumine and guide the faith of Christians in our own time.

Philosophical Hermeneutics

The word *hermeneutics* is one way of describing what we have been doing throughout this book. Hermeneutics is the art and science of interpretation. The hermeneutical process is not reserved for biblical texts. In fact, every time we read a newspaper or watch a film or attend a play, we engage in hermeneutics. The U.S. Supreme Court devotes its time and energy to interpreting legal texts in the light of the U.S. Constitution.[1] As they go about their business, the justices are engaged in hermeneutics. Musicians have only notes on a page, and actors have only written scripts. When their performances bring these texts to life, they too are engaging in hermeneutics.

In biblical studies hermeneutics, narrowly construed, refers to bringing the texts to bear on everyday life— what preachers do. Or broadly construed, it can refer to the whole process of interpreting texts—which is what this book on how Catholics read the Bible tries to do. Hermeneutics has always been an essential concern of Catholic biblical study. Catholics are not fundamentalists who imagine that they can make direct transfers from the ancient biblical texts to their lives today. Catholics are fully aware of the gaps in culture and history between the world of the Bible and our world. Catholics are also convinced that philosophy is always meaningful and important, and has a pivotal role in Catholic theology.

In the twentieth century philosophers gave a good deal of attention to hermeneutics. With the increased interest in the history of their discipline, philosophers too became readers of classic texts and often built their interpretations on those texts. What three philosophers—Hans-Georg Gadamer, Eric D. Hirsch, and Paul Ricoeur—have done in hermeneutical theory can help us to clarify the process of reading and inter-preting biblical texts. Though none of them is a Roman Catholic, their insights can help us in grasping better how the Bible has functioned and now functions in the Catholic Church.

In *Truth and Method*, Hans-Georg Gadamer illumined the processes of "pre-understanding" and "understanding" with regard to texts.[2] The term "pre-understanding" refers to the assumptions or "prejudices" that the interpreter necessar-ily brings to the object of understanding, whether it be a bib-lical or legal text, a musical score, or a script. That set of "prejudices" includes the "tradition" in which the interpreter stands (Catholic, Lutheran, Jewish, etc.), and the presump-tion that the text is a "classic," that is, one that transcends its historical circumstances and has continuing value.

In describing the process of understanding that comes about in reading a text carefully, Gadamer uses the concept of "horizon" to refer to the range of vision that includes every-thing that can be seen by a participant from a particular van-tage point. The text has its horizon, and the reader has his or her horizon. True understanding takes place in the fusion of the two horizons. Interpretation involves the sharing of a common meaning so that there is an interplay or encounter between the text and the interpreter.

Through a genuine fusion of horizons we do not remain what we were beforehand. For Gadamer, application is an inte-gral part of the hermeneutical process. And the history of the text's applications or "effects" influences how we and others look at the text. In short, the hermeneutical process is like a cir-cle that goes round and round, or better still, like a spiral that not only goes round and round but also moves ever upward.

In his essay on "Objective Interpretation" in *Validity in Interpretation,* Eric D. Hirsch took up Gadamer's concept of "horizons" and focused on the horizon of the text.[3] Hirsch defines the horizon of the text as a system of typical expectations and probabilities that were plausible in the author's context and culture. He distinguishes between meaning (what the text said in its horizon) and significance (what the text might say to people in another horizon or life-setting). He contends that the object of textual analysis is the author's meaning, and that it is possible to reach or at least approach the author's intention and the text's objective meaning though analysis of the text in its horizon.

What Hirsch proposes is what most biblical scholars do when they practice historical criticism. They investigate the meaning of the words of the text, its literary genre, and historical and cultural context. They try to arrive at a determinate actual meaning and not a mere system of possibilities, and so seek to approach the intention of the author in writing the text. While recognizing that no one can establish another's meaning with absolute certainty, they try to show that their reading is more probable than others. One of the major tasks of historical critics is to rule out some interpretations as either implausible or impossible in terms of the text's historical context. They also try to offer an account of the text that best explains the linguistic data and is consistent with the literary genres available in the historical context. Drawing out the "significance" of the text is then left to the preacher, the person at study and/or prayer, the Bible study group, and so on.

Some conservative biblical scholars have appealed to Hirsch as their hermeneutical theorist, because he seems to justify their efforts at establishing the plain or literal meaning of Scripture. However, Hirsch's approach (and the historical-critical method) is really neutral. Indeed, one can speak about the liberating character of this kind of historical criticism. After interpreters have discovered what the text meant in its horizon, they and others can then decide whether the text is significant in their horizon.

Paul Ricoeur, a French philosopher with a strong interest in biblical interpretation, is much more skeptical than Hirsch is about objective interpretation and the value of historical criticism.[4] He describes as "errors in interpretation" the attempt to recover the genius of the author, the primacy given to the original audience of the text, and the idea that there is an absolute or determinate interpretation of a text. Indeed, according to Ricoeur, the conflict of interpretations is inescapable and insurmountable.

While I am not nearly as skeptical or pessimistic about the value of historical criticism as Ricoeur seems to be, I want to call attention to some important contributions that Ricoeur has brought to our understanding of the encounter between a text and its reader. The three key perspectives carry the names of distanciation, multivalence, and appropriation.

According to Ricoeur, the very act of writing produces a distancing or alienation of the text from its author. Once written and published, the text becomes an object to be interpreted by others. It has been separated from the intention of the author and the concrete situation in which it was written. As a written and published text, it is available and open to anyone who can read it. The meaning of the text is autonomous from its author, audience, and situation because the very process of writing and making it public both objectifies and alienates, thus rendering the text a separate and new object to be interpreted.

The multivalence of a text refers to the fact that a written and published text becomes available to anyone who can read it and so becomes capable of many new readings in new situations. Since the text as it becomes a text (and is no longer merely an idea in the author's mind) transcends the situation of its production, it thus opens itself to an unlimited series of readings. Each of these readings is situated in different social and cultural conditions. This is why, according to Ricoeur, a conflict of interpretations is inevitable.

Appropriation is, according to Ricoeur, an integral part of the interpretive process, probably the most important part. Through careful analysis of the text the reader stands in relation to the kind of world that the text presents. Through interpretation of a text we as readers come to understand ourselves better in front of the text and through the medium of the text.

Ricoeur's approach to texts has been influential in providing theoretical justification for text-centered and reader-oriented biblical interpretations, which have become very popular recently. Some practitioners of literary criticism insist that the biblical text as it now stands is the proper object of interpretation. Their interest is in how the text works as a text (structuralism) and how it communicates meaning (semantics and semiotics). Other biblical interpreters are more concerned with how a text functions in the life of the reader—how the reader responds to the text, how the reader is challenged and changed by the text, and how the text might serve as a stimulus to further reflection and personal growth.

Gadamer, Hirsch, and Ricoeur represent different approaches to interpreting texts, whether biblical or other. On the theoretical or philosophical level, their perspectives are not easily reconciled. However, in practice, that may not be quite so difficult.

When I write a scholarly historical-critical analysis of a biblical text for the *Catholic Biblical Quarterly* or the *Journal of Biblical Literature* (two prominent professional journals for biblical scholars), I follow Hirsch's approach. When I prepare a homily that tries to fuse the horizons of the biblical passage and of my congregation, I follow what Gadamer proposes. When I meditate on a biblical text in the hope of learning more about myself or about what I should do, I find Ricoeur's approach helpful. The process of interpreting a biblical text is a multifaceted enterprise. The perspectives developed in philosophical hermeneutics can help us to appreciate better what we are doing when we read a biblical text.

The Literal Sense and the Spiritual Sense

All the official Catholic documents about reading the Bible insist on the necessity of investigating both the literal and the spiritual senses of Scripture. In *Dei verbum* 12, immediately after its strong endorsement of the historical and literary study of Scripture, there is an equally strong insistence on spiritual or theological reading of the Bible: "No less serious attention must be devoted to the content and unity of the whole of Scripture, taking into account the entire living tradition of the Church and the analogy of faith."

The Catholic theological tradition has always encouraged the search for both the literal and the spiritual senses of Scripture.[5] Indeed, the genius of patristic exegesis was its ability to hold both approaches in tandem, with the so-called Antiochene school stressing more the literal sense and the Alexandrian school emphasizing more the spiritual sense. From medieval times through modernity it was customary to speak about the four "senses" of Scripture: literal (the "facts" of the text), allegorical (especially what pertains to Christ), moral (what pertains to right conduct), and anagogical (what pertains to our heavenly hope, or eschatology).

However, there are problems in deciding what the "spiritual" reading of a biblical text involves. One basic problem is that how interpreters have understood and defined "literal" and "spiritual" has changed over the centuries. Moreover, in the course of time the concept of the "author" of Scripture has also changed. In biblical studies today the "author" generally refers to the human author only. But when Thomas Aquinas referred to the author and his intention, he meant first and foremost the Holy Spirit and only secondarily the human author empowered by that Spirit.

The best way to grasp what Catholics today mean by the literal and the spiritual senses of Scripture is to follow the lead of the 1993 document from the Pontifical Biblical Commission on "The Interpretation of the Bible in the Church."[6] That document defines the literal sense of Scripture as "that which has been expressed directly by the inspired human authors" (II.B.1).

This definition of the literal sense respects both the divine ("inspired") and human ("human authors") contributions of "the word of God in human language." It rejects a literalist or fundamentalist approach that claims that merely because "the Bible says so," it must be literally or historically true. Rather, the commission's document insists on the need for looking at the literary genre of the text (parable, fable, poem, etc.) and interpreting the text in its original historical and cultural context. It asserts that one arrives at the literal sense only "by means of a careful analysis of the text, within its literary and historical context."

The commission's approach to the literal sense is somewhat along the hermeneutical lines proposed by E. D. Hirsch. There are, however, some important differences. The most obvious difference is that the framers of the document regard the Bible as qualitatively different from other books, because they affirm a kind of dual human and divine origin for this book. Moreover, they hold out the possibility that a text may

have more than one literal sense (a position that Hirsch came
to endorse independently). They do so on the basis of the
"dynamic aspect" of many texts by which their literal sense
may be open to further developments produced through
"rereadings" of the text. Here the commission appears to be
moving into Ricoeur's territory. Nevertheless, it insists finally
that "one must reject as inauthentic every interpretation alien
to the meaning expressed by the human authors in their written text." Also, there is a subtle shift in emphasis brought
about in the definition through the use of the passive voice:
"that which has been expressed directly by the inspired human
author." Here the locus of meaning has shifted somewhat
from the intention of the author to the expression by
the author, and so from the author's psychology to what the
writer produced.

The Pontifical Biblical Commission's document goes on
to define the spiritual sense as "the meaning expressed by the
biblical texts when read, under the influence of the Holy
Spirit, in the context of the paschal mystery of Christ and of
the new life that flows from it" (II.B.2). This very precise
statement serves to rescue the spiritual sense from its being
construed as anything that any reader wants it to be. Rather,
following the lead of the New Testament writers and the great
patristic writers, the document takes the paschal mystery
(Jesus' life, death, and resurrection) and its appropriation by
believers under the Holy Spirit's influence as the key that
opens up the true spiritual sense of Scripture.

While the spiritual sense can never be separated from its
connection with the literal sense, the spiritual interpretation
results from setting the text in relation to the inexhaustible
richness of the paschal mystery "which constitutes the sum-
mit of the divine intervention in the history of Israel, to the

benefit of all mankind." A spiritual interpretation, according to the document, is authentic only insofar as it holds together three levels of reality: the biblical text, the paschal mystery, and the present circumstances of life in the Spirit.

An example given in the document is taken from the oracle of Nathan the prophet in which God promises to establish David's throne "forever" (see 2 Samuel 7:12–13 and 1 Chronicles 17:11–14). In Old Testament times that promise remained unfulfilled. But in view of Jesus' resurrection and Paul's claim that "Christ, having been raised from the dead, dies no more" (Romans 6:9), it is legitimate for Christians at least to find in the paschal mystery not only the true spiritual sense of the Old Testament prophecy but also its literal fulfillment in Christ.

A variation on the spiritual sense of Scripture is the "fuller sense" or *sensus plenior*. The Pontifical Biblical Commission's document defines the fuller sense as "a deeper meaning of the text, intended by God but not clearly expressed by the human author" (II.B.3). The fuller sense comes to be known when the text is studied in the light of other biblical texts that use it or in its relationship with the internal development of revelation. This latter entity is what *Dei verbum* 12 called the "analogy of faith," which refers to the inner unity among the truths of faith with one another and with Christian revelation taken as a whole.

The document gives three examples of the fuller sense: (1) The context of Matthew 1:23 ("the virgin will conceive") gives a fuller sense to Isaiah 7:14 ("the young woman will conceive"); (2) the patristic and early conciliar teachings about the Holy Trinity express the fuller sense of the New Testament texts that speak about God as Father, Son, and Holy Spirit; and (3) the Council of Trent's definition of original sin provides the fuller sense of Paul's teaching in Romans 5:12–21 about the consequences of Adam's sin for all humankind.

The Pontifical Biblical Commission's 1993 document on the interpretation of the Bible in the church has succeeded in bringing clarity into what has often seemed to be a confused area of discourse. It provides a carefully nuanced definition of the literal sense that is both faithful to the rules of historical criticism and open to the divinely inspired character of the Bible. It affirms the possibility and necessity of searching for the spiritual sense of Scripture, while insisting on the continuity between the literal and the spiritual senses. It rightly acknowledges the centrality of the paschal mystery and our appropriation of it as basic to every genuine spiritual interpretation. And it builds a bridge between Scripture and theology with its placement of the fuller sense in the context of the analogy of faith.

Scripture and Tradition

One of the slogans central to the Protestant Reformation launched by Martin Luther in the sixteenth century was *sola scriptura* ("by Scripture alone"). Luther was reacting to what he regarded as the Catholic Church's smothering of the clear message of the Bible—justification by faith alone—through human ecclesiastical traditions. In doing so he was echoing Jesus' charge against the Pharisees and their traditions surrounding the Old Testament Law: "You abandon the commandment of God and hold to human tradition" (Mark 7:8). In response to Luther the Catholic Church through its bishops and theologians at the Council of Trent insisted on the necessity of both Scripture and tradition in church life.

While some Protestants today affirm Luther's principle of *sola scriptura,* and some Catholics seem to regard Scripture and tradition as two distinct entities, the Second Vatican Council in its constitution on divine revelation, *Dei verbum*, sought to show that Scripture and tradition originate from the same source ("the same divine wellspring") and work together in Christian life: "Sacred tradition and Sacred Scripture together form a single deposit of the Word of God, which is entrusted to the Church" (*Dei verbum* 10).

Modern biblical scholarship has highlighted further the reciprocal relationship between Scripture and tradition. It has shown that Scripture is the written precipitate of traditions circulating within ancient Israel and within the early church. The Old Testament Historical Books are built up out of traditions about the patriarchs and Moses (the Pentateuch) and about leaders and kings in Israel (Joshua through 2 Kings). While the Prophetic Books bear the names of individuals (Isaiah, Jeremiah, Ezekiel, and so on), critical analysis has demonstrated that oracles and poems from various times have been collected and placed in these books. The Wisdom Books such as Proverbs (but also Ecclesiastes/Qoheleth and Sirach) represent the fusion of typical ancient Near Eastern sapiential traditions and distinctive Israelite religious perspectives.

Likewise, New Testament research has demonstrated that the Gospels developed gradually from Jesus to the Evangelists through a complex process of tradition in early Christian communities. Even Paul's letters, written primarily by one author to respond to pastoral crises within the churches that he had founded or planned to visit (in the case of Romans), contain quotations of early Christian hymns (see Philippians 2:6–11 and Colossians 1:15–20) and short credal statements. Paul also used the vocabulary and theological concepts that had already become "traditional" by the time when Paul wrote his letters in the 50s of the first century. The Bible itself is thoroughly traditional.

As we have seen, the process by which certain books became part of the canon of Christian Scripture and thus achieved the rank of "Sacred Scripture" took place largely through their use within the churches and through the efforts of bishops and theologians to specify what properly belonged to the canon of Scripture. In a real sense, the traditions of God's people created the Bible as we know it, and the Bible now serves as the guide and norm for church traditions.

What do Catholics understand by "tradition"? Since Catholic Christianity is the religion of a person (Jesus the Word of God) and not simply the religion of a book (the words in the Bible), tradition includes not only Scripture as a privileged witness to Jesus the Word of God but also "everything that helps the People of God to live in holiness and to grow in faith, and so the Church, in her teaching, life, and worship, perpetuates and hands on to every generation all that she herself is, all that she believes" (*Dei verbum* 8). In this context the apostolic preaching "is expressed in a special way in the inspired books" (the New Testament). What counts as the "deposit of faith" or tradition in Catholic circles includes not only Scripture but also the church's credal statements, liturgies, dogmatic definitions from councils and popes, and the writings of holy persons (especially the Church Fathers).

While emphasizing the unity in origin and in process between Scripture and tradition, *Dei verbum* 10 also insists that "it is not from Sacred Scripture alone that the Church draws her certainty about all revealed truth." The church is a living institution making its way as a pilgrim people within the ever-changing course of human history. Therefore it must draw upon the treasures of both Scripture and tradition to respond to the challenges of new historical circumstances.

The social teachings of the modern Catholic Church provide a good example. All the New Testament books were composed by and for Christians living under the Roman Empire. Moreover, in the first century Christians constituted a tiny minority within that empire. There was no realistic possibility for these early Christians to change the social and political systems. Nor did they show much interest in doing so. Therefore the New Testament passages pertaining to "church and state" relations are few and far between. They urge either cautious cooperation with the imperial officials (Mark 12:13–17, Romans 13:1–7, 1 Peter 2:13–17) or nonviolent resistance when the political officials demand participation in pagan rituals judged to be inconsistent with Christian faith and conscience (Revelation).

Today these biblical instructions can still be especially meaningful where Christians remain a small minority (as in China). But they can also be used to keep Christians "in line" under the control of the state (as they were in South Africa under apartheid). However, in the past 150 years, the Roman Catholic Church, drawing not only on the resources of Scripture but also on church traditions and especially on social philosophy, has issued a series of important documents on social justice.[7] While anchored in Scripture, these documents are intended to help Christians and all people of goodwill today to respond better to the changing social circumstances in which they find themselves, especially in places where Christians do have direct political authority or influence and can work effectively to bring about changes in society and culture.

In reading and studying Scripture there can be some tension between historical criticism (however indispensable it may be) and the traditional theological or spiritual interpretations of Scripture.[8] In its early manifestations historical criticism was often used in the attempt to liberate the "truth" of Scripture from church traditions and even from the traditions enshrined in Scripture itself. The nineteenth-century quest of the historical Jesus, which sought to peel away the encrustations of ecclesiastical and even biblical traditions to get back to the "real" Jesus, is a good example of that tendency.[9] The early historical critics took particular aim at the patristic allegorical interpretations of the Old Testament and of Jesus' parables, and more generally at how the Church Fathers interpreted biblical texts. To some extent the program of the early historical critics succeeded in recapturing the freshness and originality of the biblical texts. However, application of this method alone, to the exclusion of all other approaches, has often resulted in an impoverishment on the levels of theology and spirituality.

The Catholic reading of Scripture consults and respects what wise and holy interpreters over the centuries have made out of the biblical texts. All the Catholic Scripture documents single out the Church Fathers for special praise as examples of how to read the Bible spiritually and reverently. The Pontifical Biblical Commission in its 1993 document defined the particular contribution of patristic exegesis in this way: "to have drawn out from the totality of Scripture the basic orientations that shaped the doctrinal tradition of the Church, and to have provided such theological teaching for the instruction and spiritual sustenance of the faithful" (III.B.2).

One of the most fruitful developments in recent biblical scholarship has been the renewed interest in the history of biblical interpretation, or to use Gadamer's language, the effective history (*Wirkungsgeschichte* in German) of biblical texts. Both Christians and Jews have eagerly entered this field of research. Christians tend to focus on patristic writings, while Jews concentrate on rabbinic literature. Some scholars have explored the parallels or even intersections between the two interpretive traditions. The results have been the production of new critical editions and translations of the ancient texts, anthologies of the most important passages, and progress in integrating biblical criticism and early interpretations of Scripture. Special attention has been given to the religious presuppositions that the ancient interpreters brought to the biblical texts, how they solved the exegetical problems in the biblical texts, and how they used the biblical texts to address the pastoral needs of people in their own times and places.

The traditional interpretations of Scripture by the Church Fathers and the rabbis are many and varied. While we today may not want to adopt all their methods, we can and should admire their intellectual acumen, dedication to the central concerns of Scripture, and pastoral sensitivities. Their work is eloquent testimony to the inexhaustible richness of the Bible as the word of God in human language.

Questions for Reflection and Discussion

1. Do the philosophical hermeneutical perspectives of Gadamer, Hirsch, and Ricoeur help you to understand what goes on in reading and interpreting a biblical text?

2. How legitimate is it to read a biblical text through the lens of the paschal mystery? What are the dangers? What are the benefits?

3. How do you define tradition? Should there be any conflict between Scripture and tradition? Have you ever experienced such a conflict? Where and why?

What Place Does the Bible Have in Catholic Life?

"Therefore, it is right and fitting for all the preach-
ing of the Church, as indeed the entire Christian
religion, to be nourished and ruled by Sacred
*Scripture." (*Dei verbum *21)*

On practically every Sunday for almost thirty-five years I have preached on biblical texts in local parishes. I enjoy doing it, and regard it as an important aspect of my priestly spirituality. Moreover, as a professor of biblical studies on a pontifical theological faculty and an active researcher, I consider this kind of involvement in Scripture as necessary and even vital for me personally, for it challenges me to express the fruits of my learning to people who mostly do not have a formal theological education. I want to share with them the insights that I have gathered in my study of primary sources and my reading of modern scholarship on them. And I know that I must speak in ways that are intelligible and meaningful to these good people.

I prepare my Sunday sermons carefully, always trying to make clear the links that I perceive between the biblical passages and the lives of the people to whom I am preaching. Because the time allotted for a Sunday sermon in most Catholic churches in the United States is short and I want to be as concise and precise as possible, I write out my homilies, work at assimilating their content, and deliver them while maintaining eye contact with the congregation. It works for me.

In 1998 in connection with the preparations for the Jubilee Year of 2000, I prepared what I regarded as an especially good series of homilies on Luke's Gospel as a guide to Christian spirituality. As I read them over from the distance of six years in 2004, they looked very good indeed, perhaps the high point of my preaching career (such as it may be). And since other duties in my life were pressing in upon me, I decided to try a reprise of my Lukan homilies. I was sure that hardly anyone presently in the congregation would remember them. And with respect to new members, I recalled the old television slogan: "It's not a rerun if you haven't seen it before."

The results were not good. My sermon texts were objectively fine, and the topics should interest every Christian congregation. But their moment had passed. Circumstances in the Catholic Archdiocese of Boston in 2004 were very different from what they were in 1998 (due to the priest sexual abuse scandals and the closing of many parishes). And I had changed, and so had the members of the congregation. I grew increasingly dissatisfied with myself, and some of my congregants were not happy with me either. And so I abandoned my "reruns" program. The main problem was that I was not addressing effectively our new moment in 2004. I was not properly "actualizing" the Scripture texts.

The Bible has a central place in Catholic Church life today. In this chapter I want first to explain how the teaching office of the church (the Magisterium) relates to Scripture and tradition. Then I will consider the role of the Bible in ordinary Catholic life today, with particular attention to the concepts of actualization and inculturation. Finally I will explain and illustrate *lectio divina*—a simple and proven method of reading a biblical text in the Catholic tradition.

The Role of the Magisterium

In the context of Catholic theological language, the Latin word *magisterium* refers to the teaching office of the church. The Magisterium of the Catholic Church, defined formally and narrowly, consists of the body of bishops together with the bishop of Rome (the pope), teaching on matters of faith and morals. According to Vatican II's *Dei verbum* 10, "the task of authentically interpreting the word of God, whether in its written form or in the form of tradition, has been entrusted to the Teaching Office of the Church (*magisterium*), whose authority is exercised in the name of Jesus Christ." The same paragraph, however, hastens to insist that "this Teaching Office is not above the word of God but serves it by teaching only what has been handed on." In other words, the Magisterium must be guided by and serve Scripture and tradition in its decisions.

With respect to the Bible the Magisterium might function in extreme cases as an arbiter or umpire to resolve contested interpretations of texts.[1] Thus its role is analogous to that of the U.S. Supreme Court, whose task it is to decide the proper interpretation of texts in the U.S. Constitution.[2] The Magisterium does not claim to exercise its authority over issues of geography, chronology, history, authorship, and so on. However, since Catholics regard Scripture as a privileged witness to divine revelation, the Magisterium of the church has the authority and duty to make declarations about the meaning of biblical texts as they impinge on matters of faith and morals.

In coming to its decisions the Magisterium has a moral obligation to consult experts in biblical studies and theology, so as to arrive at a well-informed and defensible reading of the text in question. According to *Dei verbum* 10, the Magisterium "listens to the Word of God devoutly, guards it with dedication, and faithfully explains it." Its basic concern is not so much with deciding what the biblical text meant in antiquity (historical criticism) but rather with the implications of the text in the lives of Christians and their salvation (its spiritual sense and effective history).

In the very few instances in which the Magisterium has exercised its authority with regard to specific biblical passages, its main concern has been to counter teachings that the Magisterium has judged to be in opposition to Scripture and tradition.[3] For example, in the sixteenth century the Council of Trent, in response to claims by various Protestant Reformers about the biblical basis (or lack thereof) for the sacraments, insisted on the then-traditional connections between certain New Testament texts and the corresponding sacraments: John 3:5 ("no one can enter the kingdom of God without being born of water and Spirit") and baptism; John 20:23 ("If you forgive the sins of any, they are forgiven them") and penance or reconciliation; and James 5:14 ("Are any among you sick? They should call for the elders of the church and have them pray over them, anointing them with oil in the name of the Lord") and the anointing of the sick (or "extreme unction," as it was then called). These conciliar rulings pertained primarily to matters of then-current church life, not to the time of the Bible. They were mainly concerned with how these texts were being used in the church in the sixteenth century (their "effective history") rather than with determining exactly what the biblical authors directly intended by them.

In Catholic biblical interpretation the Magisterium, made up of the church's chief pastors, can serve as a final authority or "court of last resort." This authority has been used very, very infrequently. When used, it is intended to be carried out in a spirit of ecclesial communion, and with appropriate consultation of biblical and theological experts. The goal is greater fidelity to the gospel as this is understood from the clear statements of Scripture and the weight of church tradition.[4] Scripture, tradition, and the Magisterium are envisioned as existing in a triangular relationship. According to *Dei verbum* 10, they "are so linked and joined together that one cannot stand without the others, but all together, and each in its own way, under the action of the one Holy Spirit, contribute effectively to the salvation of souls."

The conciliar statement cited above neatly expresses the role of the Magisterium in Catholic biblical interpretation. The Magisterium may on rare occasions serve Scripture and tradition by clarifying what a biblical text means in Catholic theology and church life. The task must be carried out under the guidance of the Holy Spirit, respect the plain meaning of Scripture and the traditions surrounding it, and be done in consultation with experts. And the goal of the Magisterium's decisions about biblical texts must be to promote the cause of truth, the salvation of souls, and the good of the church.

The Bible in Catholic Life

The letter to the Hebrews is a long meditation on the early Christian confession of faith that "Christ died for us."

Making abundant use of various Old Testament texts, the author argues that Christ is not only the Son of God but also the great High Priest who offered himself willingly to expiate for our sins. The author defends his use of Scripture on the grounds that "the word of God is living and active, sharper than any two-edged sword" (3:12). The conviction that biblical texts speak not only about the past but also to the present and future is the theological basis for the prominent place that the Bible has in Catholic life.

The last chapter in Vatican II's *Dei verbum* (21–26) insists that all the Christian faithful should have easy access to Scripture, and that all preaching and teaching in the Catholic church should be "nourished and ruled by Sacred Scripture." It mandates that suitable and accurate translations be made into various languages on the basis of the Hebrew and Greek editions. It asks that annotated translations and commentaries be prepared by competent scholars, and urges that the various forms of the ministry of the word—preaching, catechesis, and religious education—be focused on and fed by Scripture. And in one of its most striking statements, *Dei verbum* directs that "the study of the sacred page [Scripture] be the soul of Sacred Theology."[5]

The practical effects of the council's directives about the Bible in Catholic life can be seen in three areas: liturgy, theological education, and ecumenism. Prior to Vatican II, the Scripture readings at Mass and other rites were in Latin and selected from a rather narrow corpus of texts. Now the readings are in the local vernacular languages (English, French, Spanish, and so on), embrace substantial parts of both Testaments, and appear in continuous sequences that allow hearers of the word to get a sense of the whole book. This means that Catholics are now exposed to large amounts of Scripture in the languages that they most readily understand.

Before Vatican II, the Bible was seldom read in any significant amount in primary and secondary school Catholic religious education programs. Instead, catechisms written at various levels provided the focus. In Catholic colleges the study of the Bible was generally guided by conservative textbooks that guided students along narrow paths. In Catholic seminaries the Bible was used mainly as a source for prooftexts in dogmatic theology, and courses in Scripture were of secondary importance. Now, however, Scripture is at the heart of all levels of Catholic religious education. Catholics have become increasingly familiar with the language and themes of Scripture, and better able to appreciate their language of worship. There has been real progress toward making the Catholic Church more "biblical" and letting the study of Scripture be the soul of Catholic theology.

Prior to Vatican II, many Catholics looked upon the Bible as a "Protestant" book. But since the council Catholics have been encouraged to claim the Bible as their book too, and what was once a source of division among Christians has turned into a force for greater unity. Both groups have become more sensitive to their shared heritage in Scripture and have come to recognize that most of their sharpest disagreements arise not from Scripture itself but rather from postbiblical developments. In Catholic circles there is enthusiasm for lectures, courses, and study groups on the Bible. Many Catholics want to know as much as they can about the Bible, and view it as an effective means in working toward great Christian unity.[6]

While Catholics today may be interested in learning what the Bible meant in its original historical setting, they are probably even more interested in discovering what the Bible might mean in their own lives. The principal task of homilists and religious educators today is to help such persons move from the biblical past to their present situations. A new way to describe this old phenomenon is "actualization." The term comes from the French adjective *actuel,* which means "present" or "contemporary." To actualize Scripture is to bring its meaning into the present time.

The Pontifical Biblical Commission's 1993 document on the "Interpretation of the Bible in the Church" (IV.A.1–3) is very helpful in explaining the actualization of Scripture. It defines actualization as the necessary task of bringing "the message of the Bible to the ears and hearts of people of our own time." The document first establishes the possibility of actualizing the Bible on the grounds of its richness of meaning and the lasting value of its message. It is a classic text—and more. Then it sets forth some methods or controls to be observed in actualizing Scripture: correct exegesis in establishing the literal sense, reading the text in light of other biblical texts, and taking the paschal mystery as the key to the text's spiritual meaning. Next it outlines three steps in the process of actualization: hearing the word from within one's own concrete situation, identifying the aspects of the present situation highlighted or put in question by the biblical text, and drawing from the fullness of meaning contained in the biblical text those elements capable of illumining and advancing the present situation in a way that is productive and consonant with God's saving will revealed in Christ.

Finally it notes some limits or obstacles that can frustrate the process of actualization: tendentious interpretations, theoretical principles (atheism, rationalism, materialism, etc.) at odds with the biblical texts, and directions contrary to justice and charity (sexism, racism, anti-Semitism). By way of conclusion the document offers this sound advice: "False paths will be avoided if actualization of the biblical message begins with a correct interpretation of the text and continues within the stream of the living Tradition, under the guidance of the Church's Magisterium" (IV.A.3).

Another new term for an old phenomenon is *inculturation.* In its theological context it refers to communicating the word of God in such a manner as to reach people in their own cultural contexts. While "actualization" concerns expressing the gospel message in the present *time,* inculturation refers more to expressing the gospel in ways and terms that are intelligible and attractive to people in a particular *place* or culture, especially one that has had little or no exposure to the Bible or the church.

Inculturation is an old phenomenon, reaching back to the earliest passages in the Bible. Think of Abraham leaving Ur for the promised land, Moses leading his people out of Egypt, the Israelites entering the land of Canaan under Joshua, the exile of Israel's religious and political leaders to Babylon in the sixth century B.C., and Diaspora Jews living all over the Roman Empire. One of the best examples of inculturation in antiquity was the production of the Greek version (the Septuagint) of the Hebrew Bible. That translation made it possible for Jews and others all over the Greco-Roman world to preserve their biblical heritage, and contributed enormously to the spread of early Christianity. The New Testament, especially in the Acts of the Apostles and in the Epistles, traces the inculturation of the movement begun by Jesus in Palestine throughout the Roman Empire. The entire history of the Christian missionary movement is the story of successful (and not so successful) efforts at the inculturation of the gospel message.

The phenomenon of inculturation is based on the Christian conviction that the gospel—the good news of Jesus' life, death, and resurrection (the paschal mystery) and its consequences for us (soteriology)—transcends the historical and cultural circumstances in which it was first revealed and now has lasting significance for peoples in every time and place.

Therefore it is necessary to find appropriate means of expressing and communicating the gospel as it comes into contact with new and different languages and cultures.

As the example of the Greek translation of the Old Testament (the Septuagint) indicates, the first and most obvious task in inculturation is translating the Bible into the languages of those who are hearing the gospel for the first time. That, however, is easier said than done. Again as the Septuagint example shows, moving from one language to another often involves a shift in conceptuality, and the process of finding the correct word to express the precise meaning of a specific biblical term is sometimes very difficult. My students from Asia and Africa frequently observe that with regard to certain biblical and theological terms, "You can't say that in my language." The fact is that one cannot translate the Bible simply on the basis of consulting a dictionary (if one exists!). Rather, translators must enter into the horizon of the other culture and come up with the proper words and images to convey the real message of the biblical texts. This situation has led to the production of "dynamic equivalence" translations (like the Good News Bible), which seek to help translators to grasp what the text means to say rather than simply what it says (formal equivalence).

Inculturation is, of course, a "two-way street." Just as the gospel influences the particular culture, so the culture influences how the gospel is proclaimed and understood. One danger is that the local culture will swallow up the gospel. Another danger is that those who proclaim the gospel will disregard and even denigrate the local culture, and try to transform it into a European or American colony.

The two sides of the inculturation "street" can be illustrated by Paul's speech in Athens according to Acts 17:22–34. On the one hand, Paul accepts and builds upon the religious culture of the Athenians. He describes them as "extremely religious" and thus wins their benevolence. He identifies their "unknown God" as the one whom he proclaims as the Creator and Lord, quotes from their pagan philosophers and poets, and urges them to accept his preaching about "a man whom he [God] has appointed" and raised from the dead (17:31). Paul shows sensitivity to the local culture, uses its language and concepts, and suggests obliquely the value of Christianity as a new and different religious option for the Athenians. Paul's speech in Athens is often proposed as a positive New Testament model for the inculturation of the gospel.

Not everyone agrees, however, with this positive reading of Acts 17:22–34. The critics (mainly evangelical Protestants) point out that this is the only place in Acts where Paul (or any other apostle) uses such an indirect approach to proclaiming the gospel. They contend that by his efforts at inculturation Paul has muted the power of the gospel. He never names Jesus, refers to him only as "a man," and slides over mention of Jesus' passion and death. And they note that, unlike the other speeches in Acts, this speech is not very successful in drawing many converts to the gospel (see 17:32–34).

My point in calling attention to this "conflict of interpretations" is that the inculturation of the gospel is a complex process. It demands ongoing evaluation and discernment if both the purity of the gospel and the positive values of the particular culture are to be preserved and enriched.

Lectio Divina

One simple and proven framework for reading the Bible in the Catholic tradition is *lectio divina*, which is Latin for "spiritual reading."[7] It is a method of reading and praying on

Scripture and other classics of spirituality such as Augustine's *Confessions* and *The Imitation of Christ*. It has deep roots in the history of monasticism. There are four basic steps in *lectio divina*: reading (What does this text say?), meditation (What does this text say to me?), prayer (What do I want to say to God through this text?), and contemplation and/or action (What difference might this text make in my relationship to God and in how I live my life?).

The text to be read can be long or short. And the full process of "reading" could take fifteen minutes or be spread over fifteen years. To illustrate the process, I will focus on Jesus' invitation in Matthew 11:28: "Come to me, all you who are weary and carrying heavy burdens, and I will give you rest." The verse is part of the larger text treated in detail in the exposition of the historical-critical method in chapter 4.

The first step, reading (*lectio*) the text, involves basic literary analysis: that is, looking at its context, words and images, characters, literary form, and structure. Here Jesus issues an invitation to come to his wisdom school, and promises wisdom and rest to those who accept. The saying is part of a passage (Matt 11:25–30) that reveals Jesus as the Son of God and incarnate Wisdom in a context (chapters 11–12) where the themes of unbelief and rejection are prominent. Appreciation of Jesus' invitation and promise grows when the passage is read alongside Jeremiah 6:16 ("where the good way lies . . . walk in it, and find rest for your souls") and Sirach 51:26–27 ("put your neck under her [Wisdom's] yoke. . . . I have labored little and found much serenity").

The second step, meditation (*meditatio*), takes account of both the content of the passage and the present dispositions of the reader. Many rich theological themes emerge from Matthew 11:25–30: real wisdom as divine revelation, the human search for wisdom and "rest," Jesus as a gentle and humble teacher, Jesus as Wisdom incarnate, and so on. What Matthew 11:28 says to me here and now will depend to some extent on my state of body and soul as I read it. I may be tired, discouraged, and depressed, and so badly in need of "rest." Or I may be feeling wonderful, hoping for a new breakthrough on the way of wisdom and more convinced than ever that true wisdom is to be found only in the teaching and example of Jesus.

The third step, prayer (*oratio*), flows from reading and meditating on the text. This step, of course, is very personal. I may ask God for peace of soul. Or I may praise God for the gift of faith and the wisdom of Jesus. Or I may thank God for having revealed himself in and through Jesus to "little ones."

The fourth step may take the form of *contemplatio* (relishing the spiritual experience and praising God for it) or *actio* (discerning some course of action). For example, through Matthew 11:28 I may decide to devote myself to learning more about the wisdom of Jesus. Or I may determine to make a retreat or to pray on a more regular basis. Or I may just take a vacation, or at least try to grasp what the rest that Jesus promises means for how I live and work.

Lectio divina is profoundly simple and eminently flexible. While rooted in monastic practice, it is also part of the heritage of Christian spirituality. It can help greatly in integrating biblical scholarship and the devotional life. It can be used with Ignatian contemplation (application of the senses and identification with the characters), especially in *meditatio*.

For individuals and groups just beginning the practice of *lectio divina*, it may be wise to follow the four-step outline rather mechanically. But I must confess that I now seldom consciously work through the various steps all in one time period. In fact, the point of *lectio divina* is to foster an immersion in Scripture so that the various questions arise naturally in their own time. For one who has been privileged to study, teach, and write about Scripture for many years, the framework has become so habitual that eventually all the steps get covered in one way or another. A wise teacher once told me: "When you have mastered a method or skill, then you can throw away the instruction booklet."

The Fathers of the Church originated *lectio divina*, with Jerome especially giving it structure. Benedict incorporated it into his monastic rule, and in the twelfth century Guigo II (the ninth prior of the Grande Chartreuse monastery) wrote an important letter on it entitled "The Ladder of Monks." While *lectio divina* never disappeared from the Christian tradition since patristic times, it has undergone a revival in large part through the efforts of the recently retired archbishop of Milan, Cardinal Carlo Maria Martini, S.J. A distinguished biblical scholar and former rector of the Pontifical Biblical Institute, Martini used *lectio divina* as a pastoral tool in his archdiocese and in his many books. Through Martini's imaginative leadership, *lectio divina* has become available to everyone not only for private devotions but also for communal Bible studies, prayer groups, and liturgical activities.

If Catholics are committed to the mandates of Vatican II to make Scripture the soul of theology and to become a more biblical church, *lectio divina* can be an effective tool tested by hundreds of years of experience. It is another case of bringing out of our biblical treasure "what is new and what is old" (Matt 13:52). While *lectio divina* is old, its use as a pastoral tool for the whole church is new and promising.

Questions for Reflection and Discussion

1. Do you see the need for the Magisterium to be involved in Catholic biblical interpretation? How would you explain its involvement to someone who is not a Catholic?

2. Do you regard Paul's speech to the Athenians in Acts 17:22–34 as a good or a bad example of inculturation? Why?

3. Can you apply the steps involved in *lectio divina* to some other part of Matthew 11:25–30 (see chapter 4)? How might this approach be helpful in your future reading of Scripture and in your prayer?

Conclusion:
Twenty-Five Theses

How do Catholics read the Bible? I am not under the illusion that most Catholics read the Bible in the ways described in this book. In fact, whenever I told friends that I was writing a book on this topic, it invariably evoked a wry comment or an anecdote to the effect that Catholics still do not read the Bible very much. Their observations generally echoed my mother's response of more than fifty years ago: "We're Catholics. We don't read the Bible."

The aim of this book, however, has been to show why and how Catholics can and should read the Bible, and to draw attention to the abundance of official Catholic documentation that offers a sophisticated and profound way of reading and interpreting Scripture. The real topic of this book has been the framework and the spirit in which the Bible can and should be read and interpreted in the context of the Catholic theological and pastoral tradition.

The following twenty-five statements can serve as both a summary of the principal points in this book and an outline of the distinctively Catholic approach to reading and interpreting the Bible:

1. From the beginning the Bible and the church have existed in a circular or symbiotic relationship.
2. The Bible is best understood as the word of God in human language.
3. Catholics follow the larger Old Testament canon adopted by the early church, while Protestants and Jews limit their canonical Old Testament to the Hebrew Bible.
4. Catholics follow the traditional twenty-seven-book canon of the New Testament along with other Christians.
5. The canonical writings serve as the rule or norm of faith and practice for Catholics, though they do not regard the Bible as the only source of divine revelation.
6. Catholics regard Scripture as a privileged witness to divine revelation and an occasion for divine revelation.
7. Catholics regard Scripture as written by human authors under the inspiration of the Holy Spirit.
8. Catholics regard Scripture as a trustworthy and inerrant guide on the road to salvation.
9. The kind of religious imagination nurtured by the Catholic tradition is especially helpful in entering into how the Bible communicates.

10. The Bible is available to Catholics in modern translations, accompanied by reliable introductions and notes.

11. Historical-critical analysis, properly understood and shorn of rationalist or positivist philosophical presuppositions, is the indispensable method for the scientific study of the meaning of a biblical text.

12. Catholics read the Old Testament for its wise teachings about God and human existence, and as preparation for and a witness to Jesus Christ.

13. Catholics view the Gospels as the product of a complex process of tradition from Jesus through the early church to the Evangelists, while providing an honest and true account of Jesus Christ.

14. Although the Gospels are not anti-Jewish in themselves, they are potentially anti-Jewish when taken out of their historical context.

15. In telling the story of the origin and growth of the church, Acts and the Epistles offer advice, consolation, and challenge to Christians in every age.

16. The Catholic reading of Scripture has been enriched by insights from philosophical hermeneutics about authors, texts, readers, and the effective history of texts.

17. The literal sense of Scripture is the meaning that has been expressed directly by the inspired human authors.

18. The spiritual sense of Scripture is the meaning that is expressed by the biblical texts when read, under the influence of the Holy Spirit, in the context of the paschal mystery of Jesus Christ and of the new life that flows from it.

19. The fuller sense of Scripture is the deeper meaning of the text, intended by God but not clearly expressed by the human author.

20. Scripture and tradition flow from the same divine wellspring, and form a single deposit of the word of God which is entrusted to the church.

21. All Catholics should have easy access to Scripture, and all preaching and teaching in the Catholic Church should be nourished and ruled by Scripture.

22. Though the Magisterium is not above the word of God expressed in Scripture and tradition, it may on occasion serve as the final arbiter in resolving conflicts about biblical interpretation pertaining to faith and morals.

23. To actualize Scripture means to bring its meaning into the present time through theology, preaching, teaching, group Bible study, various artistic expressions, and so on.

24. Inculturation involves communicating the word of God in such a manner as to reach people in their own place and cultural context.

25. *Lectio divina*—with its steps of reading, meditation, prayer, and contemplation and/or action—is a simple and proven method for reading, interpreting, and praying on Scripture in the Catholic tradition.

Appendix

Some Resources for Catholic Biblical Interpretation

Béchard, Dean P. *The Scripture Documents: An Anthology of Official Catholic Teachings.* Collegeville, Minn.: Liturgical Press, 2002. This collection of official Catholic conciliar, papal, and curial documents is the best place to go for information about the Catholic reading and interpretation of the Bible.

Bergant, Diane, and Robert J. Karris, eds. *The Collegeville Bible Commentary.* Collegeville, Minn.: Liturgical Press, 1989. This one-volume commentary on both Testaments by Catholic scholars transmits the best of modern scholarship to a wide audience.

Brown, Raymond E. *Biblical Exegesis and Church Doctrine.* New York: Paulist Press, 1985. In a series of essays Brown shows that Catholic New Testament exegesis is centrist (rather than liberal or conservative) and not destructive to Catholic doctrine.

———. *An Introduction to the New Testament*. New York: Doubleday, 1997. This synthesis of New Testament scholarship by a great expert seeks to be centrist (and not idiosyncratic) and attentive to the religious, spiritual, and ecclesiastical issues raised by the New Testament.

———. *An Introduction to New Testament Christology*. New York: Paulist Press, 1994. A reliable guide to what can be said in the light of modern biblical scholarship about how Jesus understood himself and how the various New Testament writers assessed his significance.

———. *Responses to 101 Questions on the Bible*. New York: Paulist Press, 1990. This volume answers frequently asked questions about the Bible on such topics as fundamentalism, Mary, the sacraments, and Peter.

Brown, Raymond E., Joseph A. Fitzmyer, and Roland E. Murphy, eds. *The New Jerome Biblical Commentary*. Englewood Cliffs, N.J.: Prentice Hall, 1990. This one-volume commentary on all the books of the Bible also provides topical articles on such matters as inspiration, hermeneutics, Jesus, and Pauline theology. Written by Catholic authors, it is full of reliable information and is the best example of modern Catholic biblical scholarship.

Collins, John J., and Dominic Crossan, eds. *The Biblical Heritage in Modern Catholic Scholarship*. Wilmington, Del.: Michael Glazier, 1986. The essays in this volume honoring

Bruce Vawter, one of the pioneers of modern Catholic scholarship in the United States, deal principally with the place of Catholic scholarship in the framework of contemporary ecumenical biblical scholarship.

Fitzmyer, Joseph A. *The Biblical Commission's Document "The Interpretation of the Bible in the Church."* Subsidia Biblica 18. Rome: Editrice Pontificio Istituto Biblico, 1995. An explanation of the main topics covered in the 1993 document along with extensive bibliographical information by one of the architects of the document.

———. *Scripture, the Soul of Theology.* New York: Paulist Press, 1994. The essays in this collection concern the historical-critical approach to Scripture, other approaches, Scripture as the soul of theology, and biblical study and ecumenism.

Fogarty, Gerald P. *American Catholic Biblical Scholarship: A History from the Early Republic to Vatican II.* San Francisco: Harper & Row, 1989. In tracing the story of American Catholic biblical scholarship from John Carroll to Vatican II, a distinguished church historian focuses on the struggles revolving around the acceptance of a critical and historical approach to the Bible.

Hagen, Kenneth, ed. *The Bible in the Churches: How Various Christians Interpret the Scriptures.* 3rd rev. ed. Milwaukee: Marquette University Press, 1998. Besides essays on the history of Scripture in the churches and on Scripture and ecumenism, the volume presents papers on how Scripture is interpreted in the Catholic, Orthodox, Lutheran, Evangelical, and Reformed traditions, respectively.

Harrington, Daniel J. *Interpreting the New Testament.* Rev. ed. Collegeville, Minn.: Liturgical Press, 1988. This introduction to New Testament exegesis explains in some detail the methods referred to in this book. *Interpreting the Old Testament* (1981) is similar in scope and content.

————, ed. *Sacra Pagina.* Collegeville, Minn.: Liturgical Press, 1991. This multivolume commentary on all the books of the New Testament seeks to provide sound critical analysis without any loss of sensitivity to religious meaning. The series is "catholic" in two senses: it is inclusive in its methods, and it is shaped by the context of the Catholic tradition.

The Jewish People and Their Sacred Scriptures in the Christian Bible. Boston: St. Paul Books and Media, 2002. This 2001 document from the Pontifical Biblical Commission treats the place of the Old Testament in the Christian Bible, considers basic Jewish scriptural themes and their reception in Christian faith, and examines how Jews are treated in the New Testament.

Johnson, Luke T., and William S. Kurz. *The Future of Catholic Biblical Scholarship: A Constructive Conversation.* Grand Rapids, Mich.: Eerdmans, 2002. While I find the authors' picture of current Catholic biblical scholarship too gloomy, their essays illustrate well some of the methods and concerns that are characteristic of Catholic approaches to Scripture.

Lienhard, Joseph T. *The Bible, the Church, and Authority.* Collegeville, Minn.: Liturgical Press, 1995. This book explains from a Catholic perspective the origins of the

Christian Bible and its meaning for the church today, and elaborates a Catholic understanding of the relationship among the Bible, the church, and authority.

Neuhaus, Richard J., ed. *Biblical Interpretation in Crisis: The Ratzinger Conference on the Bible and Church.* Grand Rapids, Mich.: Eerdmans, 1989. Papers by Joseph Ratzinger, Raymond Brown, William Lazareth, and George Lindbeck explore the value of historical criticism and the role of the Bible in the church.

Prior, Joseph G. *The Historical Critical Method in Catholic Exegesis.* Tesi Gregoriana, Serie Teologia 50. Rome: Gregorian University Press, 1999. This monograph argues that the historical-critical method has been and will continue to be an essential and indispensable (but limited) part of Catholic exegesis.

Schneiders, Sandra M. *The Revelatory Text: Interpreting the New Testament as Sacred Scripture.* Rev. ed. Collegeville, Minn.: Liturgical Press, 1999. This comprehensive introduction to biblical hermeneutics takes account of new ways of reading texts and shows how some traditional topics take on fresh significance when set in a different context.

Senior, Donald, ed. *The Catholic Study Bible.* New York: Oxford University Press, 1990. The first part (almost six hundred pages) consists of general and introductory articles as well as reading guides for various parts of the Bible. The second part provides the introductions, translations, and notes for the Old Testament books according to the 1970 edition of the *New American Bible* and the thoroughly revised New Testament (1988).

Stuhlmueller, Carroll, ed. *The Collegeville Pastoral Dictionary of Biblical Theology.* Collegeville, Minn.: Liturgical Press, 1996. Written by Catholic biblical scholars known for their pastoral concern, this Bible dictionary covers theological topics with reference to both Testaments and to theology and church life.

Williamson, Peter S. *Catholic Principles for Interpreting Scripture: A Study of the Pontifical Biblical Commission's* The Interpretation of the Bible in the Church. Subsidia Biblica 22. Rome: Editrice Pontificio Istituto Biblico, 2001. This excellent resource for understanding Catholic biblical study identifies twenty key principles of Catholic biblical interpretation, and discusses their meaning and significance.

Glossary

actualization: the process of bringing the significance of Scripture into the present time.

Alexandrian school: an approach to Scripture associated with the Church Fathers based in Alexandria in Egypt who focused mainly on the symbolic or allegorical significance of texts.

androcentric: pertaining to the family or social structures in which the focus is on the male (from *aner* in Greek).

Antiochene school: an approach to Scripture associated with the Church Fathers based in Antioch in Syria who focused mainly on the literal and historical meaning of texts.

biblical theology: the study of religious concepts or themes found in individual biblical texts, whole books of the Bible, or the Bible as a whole.

canon: the list of sacred writings whose content provides the rules or norms for Christian faith and practice.

canonization: the process by which the books of the Bible were recognized officially as providing the rules or norms for Christian faith and practice.

christocentric: taking the life, death, and resurrection of Jesus Christ as the center of and the key to interpreting the Scriptures.

Christology: the study of how the person, titles, and significance of Jesus have been and are now understood.

Church Fathers: Christian thinkers and leaders active especially as writers from the second to the seventh century A.D.

Congregation for the Doctrine of the Faith: the Vatican office in the Roman Catholic Church concerned mainly with clarifying and safeguarding Christian faith and practice.

Dead Sea Scrolls: the ancient Hebrew, Aramaic, and Greek manuscripts discovered at sites near the Dead Sea in the late 1940s and early 1950s.

Diaspora: the collective term for Jews living outside the land of Israel, and later applied to Christians living in the world.

dogmatic constitution: a highly authoritative statement (like *Dei verbum*) promulgated by an ecumenical council, on matters of Christian faith and life.

dynamic equivalence: the translation philosophy that is concerned with conveying the sense or meaning of biblical texts without being excessively constrained by their original wording and syntax.

ecumenical: pertaining to the whole Catholic church, and to the promotion of Christian unity throughout the world.

encyclical: an official letter on matters of faith and morals, addressed by the bishop of Rome (the pope) to other bishops, all Catholics, or (sometimes) all people of goodwill.

Essenes: a Jewish religious movement active in Israel from the second century B.C. to A.D. 70, which is generally regarded as the group behind the Qumran settlement where many of the Dead Sea Scrolls were found.

exegete: one who explains and interprets biblical texts, with attention to their literary, historical, and theological meaning.

faith and morals: the topics on which the Catholic church's Magisterium makes its official pronouncements.

formal equivalence: the translation philosophy that seeks to reflect the wording and syntax of biblical texts insofar as this is possible within the limits of good English.

fundamentalism: the approach to interpreting the Bible that stresses its inerrancy in matters not only of faith and morals but also of history and science.

gnostic: derived from the Greek word "to know," and referring to persons who claim to have esoteric knowledge about God, the world, and the human condition.

hermeneutical: pertaining to the interpretation of the meaning of texts and their significance for people today.

historical-critical method: the way of investigating biblical texts that attends especially to their original historical settings and what they meant in those contexts.

inculturation: the process of communicating the word of God in such a manner as to reach people in their own cultural contexts.

inerrancy: the understanding of Scripture as conveying without error the truth that God wished to be recorded for the sake of our salvation.

inspiration: the understanding of Scripture as written down under the guidance of the Holy Spirit.

interconfessional: involving or occurring between churches having different confessions of faith.

interdenominational: common to, involving, or pertaining to various groups within the same religion.

kingdom of God: God's reign or rule over creation, which is to be fully revealed and acknowledged at the general resurrection and last judgment.

lectio divina: a method for reading and praying on Scripture, consisting of reading, meditation, prayer, and contemplation and/or action.

lectionary: a book or list of Scripture readings to be used at liturgical services.

liberation theology: an approach to theology originating in Latin America in the late 1960s and early 1970s that emphasizes the social and political constraints upon people and looks to Scripture and theology for meaning and guidance.

literal sense: the meaning of Scripture expressed directly by the inspired human authors.

Magisterium: the official teaching office of the Roman Catholic Church consisting of the body of bishops headed by the pope as the bishop of Rome.

New Testament: the second part of the Christian Bible, consisting of the four Gospels, the Acts of the Apostles, the Epistles, and Revelation.

Old Testament: the first part of the Christian Bible, consisting of the Pentateuch, the Historical Books, the Prophets, and the Wisdom Writings.

paschal mystery: the life, death, and resurrection of Jesus Christ, and their signficance for human salvation.

pastoral: the personal advice or care offered by religious leaders to people or groups in need.

patriarchal: pertaining to family and social structures where the real power and authority are assumed to reside in the husband or father or other males.

patristic: pertaining to the Church Fathers and their writings, from the second to the seventh century A.D.

Paul: the early Christian "apostle to the Gentiles," whose missionary activity is described in Acts, and whose letters constitute a large part of the New Testament.

Pontifical Biblical Commission: the team of about twenty Catholic biblical scholars from all over the world charged with advising the pope and other Catholic Church officials on biblical matters.

postexilic: the period in Jewish history after the exile of its political and religious leaders to Babylon in the early sixth century B.C.

promulgate: to teach publicly or set forth a creed, doctrine, policy, and so on.

Pseudo-Philo: the name given to the anonymous author of *Biblical Antiquities* (in Latin *Liber Antiquitatum Biblicarum*), a selective "history" of ancient Israel from Adam to David, written in the first century A.D.

Q (Sayings Source): the (hypothetical) collection of Jesus' sayings used independently by Matthew and Luke in addition to Mark's Gospel.

Qumran: the site near the Dead Sea that was inhabited by Essenes, where most of the Dead Sea Scrolls were discovered in the late 1940s and early 1950s.

Qumran wisdom texts: the Hebrew texts found among the Qumran scrolls, the most extensive of which is called 4Q Instruction, that fit in form and content with ancient Jewish wisdom books.

rabbinic: pertaining to Jewish teachers and their teachings from the second to the seventh centuries A.D., preserved in the Mishnah, the Talmuds, and the Midrashim.

revelation: the understanding of the Bible as a witness to God's self-communication and to the decrees of God's will.

scholastic theology: the kind of philosophy and theology taught in the Middle Ages, chiefly on the authority of Aristotle, the Bible, and the Church Fathers.

Second Vatican Council: the ecumenical council of the Catholic Church held at Rome in 1962–1965.

sensus plenior: the "fuller sense" or deeper meaning of biblical texts, intended by God but not clearly expressed by the human authors.

Septuagint: the oldest Greek version of the Old Testament, traditionally said to have been produced by seventy or seventy-two Jewish scholars at the request of the Egyptian ruler Ptolemy II in the third century B.C.

soteriology: the study of salvation (*soteria* in Greek), with special reference to the effects and significance of Jesus' life, death, and resurrection for humans.

spiritual sense: the meaning expressed by the biblical texts when read under the influence of the Holy Spirit in the context of the paschal mystery of Christ and the new life that flows from it.

supersessionism: the Christian theological view according to which the church has replaced Israel as the people of God, and Israel no longer has significance in God's plan for salvation.

synod: an assembly of church leaders convoked to discuss theological and ecclesiastical affairs.

tradition: every resource that helps God's people to live in holiness and to grow in faith, as this is handed on not only in Scripture but also in creeds, liturgy, conciliar and papal definitions and decrees, and so on.

Trent: the place in Italy where an ecumenical council of the Roman Catholic Church met between 1545 and 1563 to define church doctrines and to combat the Protestant Reformation.

Notes

Chapter 1

1. All quotations and references are to the texts as presented by Dean Béchard in *The Scripture Documents: An Anthology of Official Catholic Teachings* (Collegeville, Minn.: Liturgical Press, 2002).

2. For excellent commentaries (which are also the best general treatments of Catholic biblical study today), see Joseph A. Fitzmyer, *The Biblical Commission's Document "The Interpretation of the Bible in the Church"* (Subsidia Biblica 18; Rome: Editrice Pontificio Istituto Biblico, 1995); and Peter S. Williamson, *Catholic Principles for Interpreting Scripture: A Study of the Pontifical Biblical Commission's* The Interpretation of the Bible in the Church (Subsidia Biblica 22; Rome: Editrice Pontificio Istituto Biblico, 2001).

Chapter 2

1. For a more extensive treatment, see my essay, "Introduction to the Canon," in *The Interpreter's Bible* (Nashville, Tenn.: Abingdon, 1994), vol. 1, 7–21.

2. Most editions of the *New Revised Standard Version* now provide not only the deuterocanonical books (or Apocrypha) but also several

other books contained in various Orthodox canons. See my *Invitation to the Apocrypha* (Grand Rapids, Mich.: Eerdmans, 1999).

3. The absence of Esther at Qumran has been explained in many different ways: sheer accident, the lack of references to God in the Hebrew version, "immoral" actions on Esther's part, and so on.

4. For this concept see Mary Douglas, *Purity and Danger: An Analysis of Concepts of Pollution and Taboo* (London: Routledge & Kegan Paul, 1966).

Chapter 3

1. A good reference work on these and other theological topics is *The New Dictionary of Theology,* eds. Joseph A. Komonchak, Mary Collins, and Dermot A. Lane (Wilmington, Del.: Michael Glazier, 1987). See also Carroll Stuhlmueller (ed.), *The Collegeville Pastoral Dictionary of Biblical Theology* (Collegeville, Minn.: Liturgical Press, 1996).

2. Andrew M. Greeley, *The Catholic Imagination* (Berkeley: University of California Press, 2000), 186.

3. A good example is Donald P. Senior (ed.), *The Catholic Study Bible* (New York: Oxford University Press, 1990).

Chapter 4

1. See my books, *Interpreting the Old Testament* (Wilmington, Del.: Michael Glazier, 1981) and *Interpreting the New Testament,* (rev. ed.; Collegeville, Minn.: Liturgical Press, 1988). For excellent one-volume commentaries on the whole Bible by Catholic scholars, see Diane Bergant and Robert J. Karris (eds.), *The Collegeville Bible Commentary* (Collegeville, Minn.: Liturgical Press, 1989); and Raymond E. Brown, Joseph A. Fitzmyer, and Roland E. Murphy (eds.), *The New Jerome Biblical Commentary* (Englewood Cliffs, N.J.: Prentice-Hall, 1990).

2. See Joseph G. Prior, *The Historical Critical Method in Catholic Exegesis* (Tesi Gregoriana, Serie Teologia 50; Rome: Gregorian University Press, 1999).

3. For a fuller treatment, see my commentary, *The Gospel of Matthew* (Sacra Pagina 1; Collegeville, Minn.: Liturgical Press, 1991), 166–71.

4. For a translation, see Geza Vermes, *The Complete Dead Sea Scrolls in English* (New York: Penguin, 1997), 243–300.

Chapter 5

1. See the 2001 document from the Pontifical Biblical Commission, *The Jewish People and Their Sacred Scripture in the Christian Bible* (Boston: St. Paul Books and Media, 2002).

2. See Philip J. King and Lawrence Stager, *Life in Biblical Israel* (Louisville, Ky.: Westminster John Knox, 2001).

3. For example, Robert Alter, *The Art of Biblical Narrative* (New York: Basic Books, 1981), and *The Art of Biblical Poetry* (New York: Basic Books, 1985).

4. See Vermes, *The Complete Dead Sea Scrolls in English*, 478–85.

5. See my book, *Paul on the Mystery of Israel* (Collegeville, Minn.: Liturgical Press, 1992).

6. Nobert Lohfink, *The Covenant Never Revoked: Biblical Reflections on Christian-Jewish Dialogue* (New York: Paulist, 1991).

Chapter 6

1. See Raymond E. Brown, *An Introduction to the New Testament* (New York: Doubleday, 1997).

2. See John P. Meier, *A Marginal Jew: Rethinking the Historical Jesus* (New York: Doubleday, 1991, 1994, 2001).

3. See Raymond E. Brown, *An Introduction to New Testament Christology* (New York: Paulist Press, 1994).

4. See John R. Donahue and Daniel J. Harrington, *The Gospel of Mark* (Sacra Pagina 2; Collegeville, Minn.: Liturgical Press, 2002); and Francis J. Moloney, *The Gospel of Mark: A Commentary* (Peabody, Mass.: Hendrickson, 2002).

5. See Daniel J. Harrington, *The Gospel of Matthew* (Sacra Pagina 1; Collegeville, Minn.: Liturgical Press, 1991); and Donald P. Senior, *The Gospel of Matthew* (Nashville, Tenn.: Abingdon, 1997).

6. See Joseph A. Fitzmyer, *The Gospel According to Luke* (Anchor Bible 28, 28A; Garden City, N.Y.: Doubleday, 1981, 1985); and Luke

T. Johnson, *The Gospel of Luke* (Sacra Pagina 3; Collegeville, Minn.: Liturgical Press, 1991).

7. See Luke T. Johnson, *The Acts of the Apostles* (Sacra Pagina 5; Collegeville, Minn.: Liturgical Press, 1992); and Joseph A. Fitzmyer, *The Acts of the Apostles* (Anchor Bible 31; New York: Doubleday, 1998).

8. See Raymond, E. Brown, *The Gospel According to John* (Anchor Bible 29, 29A; Garden City, N.Y.: Doubleday, 1966, 1970); and Francis J. Moloney, *The Gospel of John* (Sacra Pagina 4; Collegeville, Minn.: Liturgical Press, 1998).

9. See Joseph A. Fitzmyer, *Romans* (Anchor Bible 33; New York: Doubleday, 1993); Brendan Byrne, *Romans* (Sacra Pagina 6; Collegeville, Minn.: Liturgical Press, 1996); and Harold W. Attridge, *The Epistle to the Hebrews* (Hermeneia; Philadelphia: Fortress, 1989).

10. See my book, *The Church According to the New Testament* (Chicago: Sheed & Ward, 2001).

11. See Wilfrid J. Harrington, *Revelation* (Sacra Pagina 16; Collegeville, Minn.: Liturgical Press, 1993).

Chapter 7

1. Jaroslav Pelikan, *Interpreting the Bible & the Constitution* (New Haven, Conn.: Yale University Press, 2004).

2. Hans-Georg Gadamer, *Truth and Method* (New York: Crossroad, 1975), 235–341.

3. Eric D. Hirsch, *Validity in Interpretation* (New Haven, Conn.: Yale University Press, 1967), 209–44.

4. Paul Ricoeur, *Hermeneutics and Human Sciences* (Cambridge: Cambridge University Press, 1981), 131–44, 182–93.

5. Sandra M. Schneiders, *The Revelatory Text: Interpreting the New Testament as Sacred Scripture* (rev. ed.; Collegeville, Minn.: Liturgical Press, 1999).

6. For the text, see Béchard (ed.), *The Scripture Documents*, 244–317. For good commentaries see Fitzmyer, *The Biblical Commission's Document;* and Williamson, *Catholic Principles for Interpreting Scripture.*

7. See Thomas Massaro, *Living Justice: Catholic Social Teaching in Action* (Come & See; Franklin, Wisc.: Sheed & Ward, 2000).

8. See Richard J. Neuhaus (ed.), *Biblical Interpretation in Crisis: The Ratzinger Conference on Bible and Church* (Grand Rapids, Mich: Eerdmans, 1989).

9. Albert Schweitzer, *The Quest of the Historical Jesus: The First Complete Edition* (Minneapolis: Fortress, 2001).

Chapter 8

1. For a fine exposition, see Raymond E. Brown and Sandra M. Schneiders, "Hermeneutics," *New Jerome Biblical Commentary,* 1146–65.

2. For the similarities, see Jaroslav Pelikan, *Interpreting the Bible & the Constitution.*

3. The examples are from Brown and Schneiders, "Hermeneutics," 1163–65.

4. See Williamson, *Catholic Principles for Interpreting Scripture,* 115.

5. See Joseph A. Fitzmyer, *Scripture, the Soul of Theology* (New York: Paulist Press, 1994).

6. See Kenneth Hagen (ed.), *The Bible in the Churches: How Various Christians Interpret the Scriptures* (3rd rev. ed.; Milwaukee: Marquette University Press, 1998).

7. The following section is a slightly revised version of my essay in James Martin (ed.), *Awake My Soul: Contemporary Catholics on Traditional Devotions* (Chicago: Loyola Press, 2004), 51–56.

Index

About the Author

Rev. Daniel J. Harrington, S.J., professor of New Testament at Weston Jesuit School of Theology, has served as general editor of *New Testament Abstracts* since 1972. He did his undergraduate studies at Boston College, his doctoral work at Harvard University, and his theological studies at Weston Jesuit. He was ordained a Catholic priest in 1971 and served as president of the Catholic Biblical Association in 1985-1986. He is also the editor of the Sacra Pagina commentary series. His recent books include *Who Is Jesus? Why Is He Important?* (1999), *Why Do We Suffer? A Scriptural Approach to the Human Condition* (2000) and (with James F. Keenan) *Jesus and Virtue Ethics* (2002), all published by Sheed & Ward. He has a longstanding interest in the actualization of Scripture in antiquity and today.